BEASTS OF ALBION

BEASTS
·*of*·
ALBION

*Using Ancient British Animal Guides
for Self-development*

MIRANDA GRAY

Aquarian
An Imprint of HarperCollins*Publishers*

Aquarian
An Imprint of HarperCollins*Publishers*
77–85 Fulham Palace Road
Hammersmith, London W6 8JB
1160 Battery Street
San Francisco, California 94111–1213

Published by Aquarian 1994
10 9 8 7 6 5 4 3 2 1

A catalogue record for this book
is available from the British Library

ISBN 1 85538 318 7

Typeset by Harper Phototypesetters Limited,
Northampton, England
Printed in Great Britain by Woolnough Bookbinding Limited,
Irthlingborough, Northamptonshire

Acknowledgements

———————— ♦ ————————

My thanks to all those who have helped to develop my interest in early stories and animal archetypes, and especially to those who taught me to see the patterns and uses of card systems; to Anne Aubin, who first taught me to read the tarot, to Bob Stewart with whom I worked on *The Merlin Tarot*, and to John and Caitlín Matthews, for *The Arthurian Tarot* and for insights into Celtic shamanism. Particular thanks to my husband Richard, for his love, help and support in all my projects.

For Heather

Contents

———————— ◆ ————————

Introduction

———————◆———————

Throughout most of history, humans have lived side by side with the world of animals, sharing their territories and food sources. Animals provided vital food and warmth, and were also harnessed to share the burdens necessary for survival. Sometimes people were content merely to observe the beasts going about their own lives.

Nowadays, the vast majority of people have little contact with the animal world. Tasks that previously relied on animals' strength are now carried out mechanically; meat arrives pre-packaged on supermarket shelves; and the changes in farming methods and ever-increasing urbanization of the countryside have driven many wild beasts to areas where, if they are able to survive at all, they are rarely seen. Earlier inhabitants of Britain were much more familiar with the ways of the animals, and understood their individual habits, attributes and characteristics.

The Story-telling Tradition

Early societies relied on the spoken, rather than written, word for their communication. A major form of instruction, information exchange and moral guidance was the telling of tales and the singing of songs – epics and sagas of gods, heroes and monsters. These stories consisted of a number of archetypal images, characters, plots and artefacts. They were not just entertainment or make-believe, but carried important messages for the audience in a widely recognized form, and conveyed different levels of meaning dependent on the understanding of the listener. During the period of Celtic domination in Britain the story-telling tradition was particularly strong. Stories were given a formal structure and formed part of the teaching and instruction process of the druidic religion, whose formal hierarchy included the ranks of bard, ovate and druid. The tradition continued in Britain through the waves of invasions by Romans, Saxons, Danes and Normans, throughout the medieval period when a body of stories and myths were used by the Church as both moral instruction and warning, through the writings of poets such as Shakespeare, Milton, Spenser and others, and even into the Victorian age in folk song, nursery rhyme and children's stories.

In many of these tales, animals, familiar companions or recognizable figures, would be used to represent a particular concept or archetype that the listener could understand without further explanation. A character associated with a fox, for example, would be sly and cunning, while the appearance of a white stag would herald Otherworld forces or an imminent adventure in the Underworld.

Many stories make use of the theme of magicians, heroes or otherworldly beings who have the ability to transform themselves into the shape of one or more animals. Several tales feature magical duels between shape-changers, each of whom takes on the form of a new beast – more potent than the last – to threaten or triumph over the opponent. Other stories tell of swan-maidens, werewolves or enchanted pigs – ordinary mortals who are either transformed into animals through punishment, accident or malice, or who can take on the shape of the beasts at will, living part of their lives in human form and part as beasts. These transformations represent the acquisition of the strengths and attributes of that particular animal by the initiate – the person who has attained the necessary knowledge and understanding to do this. The advantages and consequences of this action would be explored in the plot of the story.

Furthermore, those who heard the tale and interpreted its message understood how to take hold of the power of the animal and apply it to their own circumstances. Many tribes, clans and individuals looked to 'totem animals', whose attributes represented aspects of their own character and who could be called upon as needed to guide and protect.

The last century has seen an increase in mass communication

and the spread of literacy, which have all but hidden the original archetypal animal images from modern readers. The animals themselves are no longer so familiar or well-understood. These images have nevertheless been handed down to us in the forms of old stories and legends, songs and rhymes, and show a remarkable uniformity of interpretation. The medieval art of heraldry, carried forward even today in coats of arms, emblems and logos, contains many echoes of the earlier animal archetypes in the way in which animal images are used. Today's successors to the old tales are the Walt Disney cartoon and the television puppet; but even here, and in works of literature such as Kenneth Grahame's *Wind in the Willows* and Lewis Carroll's *Alice* stories, animal archetypes can be found, albeit in many cases distorted almost out of all recognition from the original representations. Some stories have been taken to other countries in the waves of emigration from Britain, and have been adapted into local forms. In some cases, thanks to modern communications and media, these altered forms have returned to Britain, and are now perhaps more familiar than the originals to modern listeners and viewers. The television has taken the place of the story-teller, and most people's archetypes are now shaped by the cartoon and the wildlife documentary.

Albion

Early Greek writings tell of trade with the northern islands of 'Albion' and 'Ierne' – mainland Britain and Ireland respectively. Pliny also referred to Britain as 'Albion', and Nennius suggested that the name may be derived from the name of a local goddess, 'Albina', or 'The White One'. Another suggestion was that the name was coined by the Romans from the Latin 'albus', or 'white', from the white cliffs on the south coast which would have been the first sight of the islands for many travellers, although this is probably a justification rather than an origin, because of the earlier Greek references. The name 'Albu' was used by the Irish to refer to mainland Britain until at least the 10th century.

One legend tells that the first inhabitants of the islands of Britain were a race of giants whose king, 'Albion', gave his name to the land. A similar tale is told by Geoffrey of Monmouth in his *History of the Kings of Britain*. According to Geoffrey, the Trojan hero Brutus and his followers, exiled and searching for a new land to settle, landed in Totnes to find the island known as 'Albion' inhabited by giants. Brutus wrestled with the king of the giants, known as Gog-Magog, and succeeded in throwing him into the sea. Thereafter the land was renamed 'Britain' in honour of Brutus.

In *Beasts of Albion*, the term 'Albion' is used loosely to represent all the various peoples who have lived in or influenced the *group identity* of the islands known as Britain, including Ireland and, at some stages of history, 'Little Britain' on the European mainland, now known as Brittany. Thus the term is not intended to refer to a specific bounded geographic area, but rather a body of lore and tradition which found a home in the islands which developed into the area now known as Britain. The stories in this book come from Greek and Roman legend; Celtic and Saxon tales, both from Britain and continental Europe; Norse and Teutonic myth; and medieval church beliefs, as well as the local stories centring around a particular monument, town or location.

Many stories have their roots in one or more of the major religions which were prevalent in the islands, from the gods and heroes of the Romans, Celts and Vikings to the early Christian church. The major criterion for inclusion has been that the legend, rhyme, story or image must have been familiar to at least some of the inhabitants of the islands we now call Britain at some time in the past or present. Where possible, the origin of the story has been indicated, whether Welsh, Irish, Breton, Norse, Saxon etc. In many cases, however, similar stories occurred in several different areas, and the geographical limits have blurred at the edges.

The Beasts

The animals chosen for the cards in *Beasts of Albion* are – or once were – native to Britain. They are the beasts that appear most often, or as the strongest images, in folklore. The ancient archetypes of these once-familiar British animals are re-examined in the book by exploring their role in stories, legends and folk tales. By relating these archetypes to modern situations and problems, you will rediscover the ability to make use of the power of the animal in order to learn and grow, and to capture the essence of each beast in the development of the Inner Self – that level of awareness which lies below everyday consciousness and experience.

All the attributes of the featured animals lie within each individual; at certain times some of those characteristics emerge more strongly than others. These strengths and abilities can be called upon and accessed in time of need by using the cards as a focus for meditation or visualization, in order to remind yourself of your own true abilities and potentials.

Using the deck and this book, you will be guided to encounter your own 'Totem Animal' – the one beast whose attributes represent your inner character and characteristics, the one who will normally share your story throughout life. You will also discover a number of 'Companion Animals', who may be encountered from time to time to offer their strengths to help you cope with particular problems or situations. Using the structure of the Spiral Path you can develop your own path of gradual awakening and transformation by encountering and sharing the stories of each animal in turn.

The Cards

When you first open the deck, take time to go through each card, studying carefully the image and designs. Keep a notebook with you to record any initial thoughts about each animal that come to mind. Be aware of your immediate reaction to the animal, any stories, legends or superstitions you know concerning the beast, and any characteristics or attributes you feel the animal displays, either from your own knowledge of it or from the image on the card. Keep the notebook with you whenever using the deck, and use it to record your experiences and discoveries as you go along.

The cards are divided into three Kingdoms: Strength, Knowledge and Purity. A Spirit Animal represents each Kingdom:

Lion, Dragon and Unicorn respectively. The Kingdom for each animal can be identified by the colour of the vertical border on the card: reds for Strength, greens for Wisdom and blues for Purity. Lay out the deck in the three Kingdoms, with the appropriate Spirit Animal at the top of each one.

KINGDOM OF STRENGTH

Spirit: The Lion

Principle	Position 1	Position 2	Position 3
GROWTH	Mouse	Squirrel	Snake
CHALLENGE	Boar	Hound	Raven
INTELLIGENCE	Weasel	Fox	Wren
CREATION	Bee	Horse	Spider

KINGDOM OF WISDOM

Spirit: The Dragon

Principle	Position 1	Position 2	Position 3
AWAKENING	Bear	Cockerel	Bat
EMPOWERING	Bull	Brock	Stag
PROTECTION	Hedgehog	Goose	Crane
KNOWLEDGE	Owl	Cat	Salmon

KINGDOM OF PURITY

Spirit: The Unicorn

Principle	Position 1	Position 2	Position 3
COMPASSION	Dolphin	Wolf	Redbreast
NURTURING	Otter	Cow	Pig
INSPIRATION	Hare	Swan	Eagle
TRANSFORMATION	Toad	Dove	Butterfly

Fig. 1: The Three Kingdoms

Within each Kingdom, the beasts are grouped into sets of three, or 'Trines'. Each beast within a Trine represents a different 'harmonic' of the same principle; that is, the principle itself is the same in each case, but the manner in which it is perceived and applied will vary. In the Trine of Nurturing, for example, each animal represents a different aspect of nurturing. The Otter relates this concept to the Self, in developing joy within your own character, the Cow relates it to Others, in providing nurturing and sustenance for other people, and the Pig represents nurturing on a spiritual plane, awakening others to knowledge and enlightenment. Cards depicting animals within the same Trine will have identical top borders. Group the cards within each Kingdom into the four Trines, using Fig. 1 to find the major principle for each.

Each Trine may be laid out in the form of a triangle, as in Fig. 2. Position 1 represents the lowest harmonic of the principle, as it relates to the Self. Position 2 represents the Inner Self, and Position 3 is the highest harmonic, representing matters Beyond the Self. Place the cards for each Trine within the triangle shapes, with positions as indicated in Fig. 1.

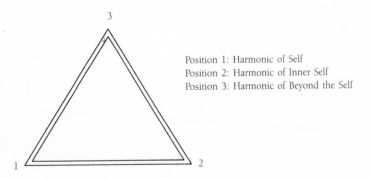

Position 1: Harmonic of Self
Position 2: Harmonic of Inner Self
Position 3: Harmonic of Beyond the Self

Fig. 2: Harmonics of the Trine

You may feel that a particularly important animal is missing from the deck, or that you would prefer to replace one of the images with an alternative beast with particularly important attributes and associations for you. If so, use the blank card to make your own image. Find a suitable picture of the desired animal, perhaps a photograph, print, drawing or icon, which seems to display the major strength of that animal. Paste this image onto the blank card and use it alongside the rest of the deck. Decide where the 'new' animal should fit within the structure of Kingdoms and Trines.

You now have the basic structure for working with the cards. The Spiral Path allows you to encounter each animal in turn, starting with the lowest harmonic of Self in the lower Kingdom of Strength, and working your way through each Trine until you reach the highest harmonic of Beyond the Self in the highest Kingdom of Purity. More details on how to follow the Spiral Path are given in Part 4.

Part 1 is a guide to the principles and significance of each animal, based on the stories, myths and legends of earlier inhabitants of Albion. The first section gives some examples of major stories in which the beast appears; the second section summarizes the main characteristics of the animal as demonstrated by the stories and the animal's own natural habits; and the third section indicates the teaching which the animal is likely to bring when encountered on the Spiral Path.

Please bear in mind that my suggestions are not intended as a definitive interpretation of each animal's meaning, but rather to guide and encourage you to bring out your own experiences, feelings and interpretations. Working with the beasts is an intensely personal experience, and it is important for you to develop your own patterns and paths with the cards.

The Beasts of Albion lie within you, and offer guidance and companionship, strength and knowledge along the path of self-discovery and growth.

PART 1

———————◆———————

The Animal Guides

Mouse

◆

KINGDOM: Strength

TRINE: Growth

TEACHING: Seeker of the Path

MYTHOLOGY AND FOLKLORE

The Mouse is often depicted as weak and timid, but with compensating attributes of intelligence, resourcefulness or compassion. It is a symbol of how weakness may be turned to strength, as in the common modern cartoon myth of the Mouse being the only animal that can frighten an elephant, and Aesop's fable of the lion and the Mouse. The story originally concerned a lion and a rat, but the Mouse has become more widely recognized in this role. One day, a Mouse popped out of its hole to find itself right between a lion's paws. Instead of eating the Mouse, the lion magnanimously let it go free. Later the lion was trapped in a hunter's net, and the Mouse, on hearing its calls for help, ran to gnaw through the rope, setting the beast free.

In earlier times, the Mouse was regarded as a manifestation of the human soul, and a vehicle by which the soul could leave the sleeping body and travel around at great speed. Because of their habits of living underground and in dark places, Mice were regarded as creatures who travelled between the world of men and the Underworld; but as creatures associated with the harvest and the sun, they were also a symbol of abundance and wealth, and were associated with Apollo, the Roman god of light, as well as with deities of the harvest.

Like their larger cousin the rat, Mice could provide warning of death or disaster; if they suddenly left a house or ship for no obvious reason, bad luck and death would soon follow. A sure sign of imminent death was a mouse running over a person, particularly if the individual was already sick. Mice were used in remedies, and those involving eating the animal's flesh were held to be particularly effective against many ailments including whooping cough, measles, fits and warts. Mice were respected for their strong, sharp teeth, and in some places a child's milk teeth would be placed in a mouse-hole in the hope that the adult teeth that followed would take on the virtues of the Mouse teeth.

Mice were renowned for travelling along secret paths, and finding routes through even the tiniest gap to gain access to a food source or to escape from danger. They were reviled, however, for their destructive habits, which could be out of proportion to their small size; harvests or stores could be ruined by the ravages of these creatures, and some Christian myths used the symbol of a Mouse to depict the devouring Satan, chewing on the roots of the Tree of Life.

In the Welsh story of the *Mabinogion*, Manawydan, step-father of the hero Pryderi, was tormented by a devouring band of Mice while trying to raise crops in the land of Dyfed which, due to an enchantment, was empty of all people save Manawydan himself and Pryderi's wife Cigfa. Manawydan and Cigfa farmed three fields of wheat, which grew in magnificent abundance with huge, ripe heads; but before they could harvest the first two fields, they found that the crop had been ravaged, with every ear of wheat taken.

On the night before he was due to harvest the third field, Manawydan kept watch over the field all night, and in the darkest hour he saw a horde of huge Mice descend upon his field and devour all of the carefully nurtured crop. Manawydan chased the Mice but they were all too fast for him except one, which he caught in his glove. In a fury, Manawydan took the Mouse back to Cigfa, and began to erect a tiny scaffold on which he intended to hang the Mouse as a thief.

As Manawydan was working on the scaffold, a series of holy men – the first humans to have been seen in the land of Dyfed since the enchantment began – rode up and rebuked Manawydan for stooping so low as to hang a Mouse, offering him increasing amounts of money to release the beast; but Manawydan was adamant. The final visitor was a richly adorned bishop with his full retinue. Manawydan knew that these priests were not what they seemed, and he bargained with the false bishop to release the land from its enchantment and free the people. The bishop revealed himself to be Llwyd, whose family had held a grudge against Pryderi, and who had placed the enchantment in an act of revenge. The Mice were Llwyd's war-band, and the one Manawydan had captured was his pregnant wife. In return for the freedom and restoration of the Mouse, the enchantment was lifted and all the people restored.

CHARACTERISTICS: *Resourcefulness; Intelligence; Timidity; Anxiety; Uncertainty; Compassion; Fertility; Industriousness; Abundance; Wealth; Destructiveness*

In a spread, the Mouse represents the ability to find hidden solutions to problems, perhaps by harnessing apparent weaknesses and turning them into strengths. It may also signify a lack of self-confidence and a tendency to worry. The Mouse's industry may lead to wealth and abundance, but if allowed to remain uncontrolled and excessive may turn to destruction.

SPIRAL PATH MEANING: *SEEKER OF THE PATH*

The Mouse is the guide to your path in life. It knows the hidden forces that pull you, and will help to seek for the path you must follow.

Squirrel

KINGDOM: Strength

TRINE: Growth

TEACHING: Pivot of the Worlds

MYTHOLOGY AND FOLKLORE

The Squirrel is generally regarded as a mischief-maker – perhaps because of its habit of sitting on an out-of-reach branch or vantage point and 'scolding' anything that passes by with the distinctive noise it makes when disturbed or agitated.

In Scandinavian mythology, the Squirrel Ratatosk sits in the Tree of Life, Yggdrasil, and carries messages between the eagle perched at the top of the tree and the serpent coiled at its roots. In some interpretations, this gives the Squirrel the ability to 'run the gauntlet' between good and evil; and in some shamanic traditions it symbolizes the journey of the shaman between Underworld, Middle World and Overworld. An alternative view is that the Squirrel is actually stirring up trouble between the eagle and the serpent, thus reinforcing its 'mischief-maker' image. Perhaps it is therefore just as well that the Squirrel was said to enjoy the special protection of the god Thor.

An old Christian tale tells that the Squirrel originally had a long, thin tail like a rat. Sitting in a tree in the Garden of Eden, the Squirrel observed Adam and Eve eating the forbidden fruit, and was so horrified at this disobedience that it drew its tail across its eyes to blot out the sight. As a reward for this faithfulness, the Squirrel was given the thick, bushy tail it now bears.

In Irish tradition, the Squirrel was the familiar beast of the goddess Maeve. To kill a Squirrel – or in some cases simply to pass under a branch where one is sitting – was regarded as bad luck, and could result in an accident or in the loss of a hunter's skill. The Squirrel's well-known habit of carefully storing a cache of nuts has been seen in some quarters as a sign of greed, but in others as prudence and forward planning.

CHARACTERISTICS: *Resourcefulness; Quick Intelligence; Bravado; Mischief; Communication; Forward Planning; Practicality; Prudence; Enjoyment*

In a spread, the Squirrel represents the ability to balance the mundane demands of life with higher intellectual and spiritual needs, although the spiritual side may be hidden beneath a seemingly shallow exterior. It can represent easy and free communication, although there may be a tendency towards gossip or mischievous interference. The Squirrel's apparent carefree enjoyment of life does not prevent it from making prudent and practical preparations for the future.

SPIRAL PATH MEANING: *PIVOT OF THE WORLDS*

The Squirrel teaches growth through communication, and shows how to balance the needs of the upper, spiritual levels; the middle, mundane levels; and the lower, subconscious levels of the self.

Snake

◆

KINGDOM: Strength

TRINE: Growth

TEACHING: The Path of Change

MYTHOLOGY AND FOLKLORE

The Snake's unusual natural habits almost certainly account for much of its symbolism in stories and folklore. The regular shedding of the old skin represents new life or regeneration; the venom of the adder (the only poisonous Snake in Britain) represents danger and guardianship; and the Snake's habit of living underground reinforces its link with the Underworld, with death and with chthonic forces. The strange sinuous movement of the Snake on land and water sets it apart from other animals, and its multiple penises, reproductive propensity and phallic shape make it a natural symbol of virility and fertility. As a result, the serpent has been held in great reverence and awe throughout history, and appears frequently in iconography of many kinds.

Among the Romans, the Snake was generally regarded as a beneficent spirit, and pet Snakes were often encouraged to stay in the house as guardians (although this was probably rare in the cold northern outpost of Roman Britain). Snakes were particularly identified with the healer god Asclepios, who took the form of a Snake while ministering to victims of a plague in Rome; and with other Roman healer gods and goddesses. The two intertwined serpents on the Caduceus, the familiar universal symbol of medical healing, stem from this association. In the Mithraic cult, the Snake is also represented as protective, travelling with the God Mithras alongside his horse and, with the dog, lapping up the blood of the sacrificed bull.

Snake symbolism is extremely widespread in Celtic relics. Many gods and goddesses, especially those associated with healing or with water, are depicted in the company of the beasts, in some cases to the extent that the deity's limbs are depicted as Snake bodies. The goddess Brigid, patroness of childbirth, is associated with Snake worship, and there are some indications that early temples and sites such as the one at Avebury in Wiltshire may also contain elements of Snake symbolism. 'Snake-stones', said to be formed by adders breathing onto a hazel wand, were used by the druids for divination and were also said to have healing properties.

The ram-headed Snake is a particularly important image, and features in many Celtic torcs and neck-rings. This symbol is also closely associated with the horned god Cernunnos, an extremely powerful and enduring icon. The guardian serpent also appears in many Celtic legends, as does the monster Snake as a trial that must be overcome by heroes such as CuChulainn, Fionn and Conall Cernach.

Medieval folklore, while fearing the Snake for its venom, nevertheless kept the link with healing. Adder stones, said to be formed from the skin of fighting adders, were used for healing cataracts in the eyes. The dried heads of Snakes were rubbed onto a wound to cure snake-bite, and their skin would be worn around the head to prevent headaches or around the limbs to fend off rheumatism. An adder's venom was used to induce abortion.

The image of the Snake as tempter or betrayer is familiar through the story of Adam and Eve in the Garden of Eden, but also has other local echoes. At King Arthur's last great battle of Camlan, a truce had been declared so that Arthur and Mordred could parley, and perhaps avoid the battle altogether. As the two parties talked, however, one of Arthur's knights spotted an adder in the grass at the king's feet, and drew his sword to slay it. Mordred's army saw the flash of the unsheathed sword as a sign of Arthur's betrayal, and the terrible battle began.

The slaying of the serpent has symbolized for many cultures the triumph of light over dark, or in later times the victory of Christianity over the pagan cultures. Apollo slew the monster

Python at Delphi; St George and St Michael are both depicted as slaying dragons or serpents as representations of the repression of older religions, or as the containment of the forces of chaos. St Patrick is said to have banished the Snake from Ireland, and in Christian iconography the Snake is often depicted at the foot of the cross. Even at a more humble level, the superstition persisted that to kill the first adder seen in the springtime would bring good luck throughout the year, while to let it escape would surely bring disaster.

CHARACTERISTICS: *Regeneration; Healing; Luck; Renewal; Secret Wisdom; Fertility; Guardianship; Power of Nature; Life Force; Catalyst; Sexuality; Untrustworthiness*

In a spread, the Snake represents a growth process through several successive stages. It can also mean regeneration, the ability to renew your energies and to heal yourself, or it may signify change which is necessary, however painful it may prove to be. The Snake has the ability to grow – to achieve great changes through a series of smaller steps.

SPIRAL PATH MEANING: *THE PATH OF CHANGE*

The Snake teaches the cycles of growth and decay. It offers growth through the successive stages of life and experience, outgrowing and destroying old ideas, values and perceptions and enabling the generation of new ones.

Boar

◆

KINGDOM: Strength
TRINE: Challenge
TEACHING: Challenge of Life

MYTHOLOGY AND FOLKLORE

The wild Boar, once widespread in the forests of Britain but now no longer found in the islands, was greatly respected throughout the land for many centuries. Hunting was the major preoccupation of warriors in peacetime, and hunting the wild Boar brought particular status, involving as it did a personal confrontation with a fierce, daring and powerful opponent, with a realistic risk of serious injury for the inept or careless. Pig flesh was a staple food for early man, with the choicest cut of meat, the 'Champion's Portion', being reserved for the bravest hunter or warrior. Small wonder then that symbols of the Boar – particularly with its bristles raised for battle – are widely found in the battle gear and weaponry of several cultures that dominated Britain, and stories featuring the beasts were numerous.

In the Irish stories of Fionn mac Cumhal, the hero Diarmaid meets his death at the hands of a magical Boar. Diarmaid had stolen the ageing Fionn's betrothed, Grainne, and was pursued throughout the land. After seven years, however, Fionn appeared to forgive the lovers, and invited them back to court. But Fionn was still bent on revenge, and tricked Diarmaid into taking part in a Boar-hunt. The quarry was the 'Earless Green Boar of Ben Gulbain' – in fact Diarmaid's foster-brother, magically trans-formed, and which Diarmaid was forbidden to hunt under his personal geas (a prohibition or constraint in Celtic society, the penalty for the breaking of which was loss of honour or status, disastrous bad luck or even death). Diarmaid succeeded in killing the Boar, but was pierced in the heel by one of its poisoned bristles. Diarmaid begged Fionn, who was nearby, for a magical healing drink, but Fionn, in a final act of revenge, allowed the water to drip through his fingers onto the ground, and Diarmaid died.

Boars – and in particular the legendary, monstrous Boar named Twrch Trwyth – are also intimately bound up in the Welsh story of Culhwch and Olwen. The name 'Culhwch' means 'pig-sty', and was conferred on the unfortunate hero when his mad mother gave birth to him in a pig-sty, having been terrified by pigs. After the death of his mother, Culhwch's step-mother insisted that he should marry Olwen, the daughter of the giant Yspaddaden. Before giving his consent, however, Yspaddaden insisted that Culhwch should carry out 39 impossible tasks, the chief of which was to obtain the comb and scissors resting between the ears of the monster Twrch Trwyth. This Boar was a former king who, along with his followers, had been magically transformed to animal shape, and had been roaming the length and breadth of the country causing great destruction. Accompanied by the divine Mabon and the legendary King Arthur, Culhwch hunted the Boar throughout the kingdom, and finally recovered the comb and scissors (which represented Ogham characters of knowledge and transformation).

The Scandinavian invaders also found great reverence for the Boar, holding it sacred to their gods Frey, Freyja and Odin. The Boar was sacrified to Frey at the Yule festival, when the god was believed to ride the golden bristled boar Gulliburstin, whose bristles formed the sun's rays. Boar adornments on shields, helmets and other war-gear placed a warrior under the protection of Frey. Solemn oaths were sworn by the golden Boar as a protection against falsehood, and until comparatively recently, giving a person a meal of pig's brains was reputed to make him or her speak only the truth.

The Boar's head is held to be the seat of its power and protection, and formed a popular and traditional Yuletide dish in medieval times, still remembered in the 'Boar's Head Carol' popular today. The beast is particularly associated with regions that maintain strong Celtic influences, especially Cornwall.

CHARACTERISTICS: *Daring; Ferocity; Challenge; Bravery; Physical Strength; Stamina; Abruptness; Vitality; Truth; Directness; Anger*

In a spread, the Boar represents the strength of character to advance, either in pursuit of some goal or in making others see your point of view. It can mean a bold and daring attitude towards life, but also comes with a warning of potential for destruction. The Boar places great importance on the truth and directness, and will not suffer fools gladly.

SPIRAL PATH MEANING: *CHALLENGE OF LIFE*

The Boar teaches the physical challenges of life. By hunting him you overcome obstacles in your life, thereby gaining the strength, confidence and wisdom to take the treasures of knowledge and transformation from between his ears.

Hound

KINGDOM: Strength
TRINE: Challenge
TEACHING: Challenge of Loyalty

MYTHOLOGY AND FOLKLORE

Hounds and other dogs have enjoyed one of the longest associations with mankind of any beast. They have acted as faithful companion, guard, guide and fearsome opponent. Hounds appear in many stories in all of these roles, and it is important to recognize which archetype is being used in any particular instance. Fairy dogs, or Hounds of the Underworld, were typically pure white with red ears and eyes. They were commonly used as guides into the realms of faerie, and to follow them led the unsuspecting into adventures in the Underworld. Huge black dogs with glowing red eyes and salivating jaws were monsters to be overcome, sometimes as the guardians of a treasure or a path. Black dogs roaming hillsides or moors were often spectral, and presaged death or disaster.

Many gods and heroes had dogs associated with them, either as representations of their own attributes, or as guides and helpers on their quests. Hounds were particularly associated with mother–goddess figures, and with the deities Epona, Sucellos, Nodens and Woden among others. King Arthur had a faithful hunting Hound named Cabal, who assisted him in the quest for the monster boar Twrch Trwyth; the Irish hero Fionn mac Cumhal had two favoured Hounds named Bran and Sceolan, who were actually his nephews transformed. The Irish god Lugh had a magical Hound who could not be overcome in combat, and whose bathing water would turn to wine. But the hero with the closest association with the Hound was the Ulsterman, CuChulainn.

In his youth, CuChulainn was known by his given name, Setanta, and was raised at the court of his uncle Conchobar, king of Ulster. One day, Conchobar and his court were invited to a feast by the smith Chulainn, whose property was guarded by a huge and vicious Hound. Arriving late at the feast, Setanta was attacked by the dog, and killed it by hurling his shinty ball right down the beast's throat and through its body. Chulainn, however, was devastated by the loss of his companion and guard. In recompense, Setanta offered to rear the Hound's puppy personally until it was old enough to take the old dog's place; and in the meantime to assume its role as guardian and protector himself. Ever afterwards, he was known as Cu Chulainn, 'the hound of Chulainn'.

CuChulainn derived not only his name from a dog, but also his downfall. Because of his close association with the Hound, CuChulainn had a geas laid upon him that he should never eat dog flesh. Unfortunately, another condition was that he should never refuse an offer of hospitality; so when, approaching his final battle, CuChulainn was invited by three old crones at the roadside to share their meal of roasted dog, he had no option but to agree. As soon as he had eaten the flesh of his totem animal, CuChulainn's strength and battle skills were weakened, and he was overcome.

The Welsh god of the underworld, Arawn, had a pack of magical white Hounds with red ears called the Cwn Annwn, or 'Hounds of Hell'. The hero Pwyll came across these Hounds in pursuit of a stag, and beat them off to claim the kill as his own. As a punishment, Pwyll had to live in the Underworld for a year and defeat Arawn's enemies. In Norse myth, the road to hell was guarded by a monster dog named Garm – a very close echo of Cerberus, the three-headed guardian of Hades in Greek myth.

In some stories, the road to the Underworld is through water, and packs of Hounds may lead the traveller into a pool, river or sea, where they 'drown', or enter the Underworld. The Celtic sea-god Manannan kept such a pack, which he used to hunt a monster pig. The Irish goddess Aine had a stone, Cathar Aine, at which all the mad dogs in Ireland would gather before plunging into the sea.

Many legends throughout Britain and Europe tell of the 'Wild Hunt', a supernatural pack of Hounds who can fly through the air at night in pursuit of their quarry. The Hunt – known by the Saxons as Einherier or Herlathing, and in different parts of the country as the Gabriel Hounds, Wisht Hounds or Dartmoor Hounds – is an abiding and terrifying image. The leadership of the Hunt has been variously ascribed to Gwyn ap Nudd, Woden, Herne the Hunter, King Arthur, Charlemagne and the Devil. The prey may be a white boar or stag, white-breasted maidens or the souls of the damned. One version claims that the Hounds themselves are actually the souls of unbaptized children. Another story tells that a small black dog from the Hunt could occasionally be left behind accidentally. Bad luck would follow if this Hound were not fed and looked after for a year, before being reclaimed by the Hunt.

Hounds frequently featured in early ritual burials and sacrificial rites, and even into medieval times were often buried under the doorways or in the walls of new buildings so that their spirit would protect the house. Dogs could reputedly see ghosts, and would give warning of supernatural danger. There are also many stories of dogs being able to sense the impending death of their owners, or to foretell disaster and misfortune. On the other hand, there are the many legends of monstrous spectral dogs roaming the moorlands and hills and attacking travellers – a theme carried through into Sir Arthur Conan Doyle's famous *Hound of the Baskervilles*.

Despite its fierceness, the dog has also had a long association with healing, being a companion of both the Greek Asclepios and the Celtic healer-god Nodens. A dog's saliva was held to have curative properties. In the early, traditional 'Corpus Christi' carol, a king lies wounded upon his bed, guarded by a faithful Hound at his feet licking the blood from his wounds – a Christian adaptation of the earlier belief symbols of both guardianship and healing. In the Roman Mithraic religion, the symbol of the lapping dog is also seen, along with the snake, licking up the blood of the sacrificial bull.

CHARACTERISTICS: *Loyalty; Trust; Companionship; Faithfulness; Guardianship; Instinct; Enthusiasm; Healing*

In a spread, the Hound represents the qualities of faithfulness, loyalty and companionship. It can signify a loyalty that bonds heart and soul beyond intellectual reason, even if the object of the loyalty is not worthy. It may also represent healing derived from self-trust and faith in personal abilities. The Hound will fiercely protect those to whom it is loyal, but its actions and motives may be driven by the desire or need for praise and reward. As a pack animal, the Hound may be led into rash or unwise actions because of the desire for respect from its peers.

SPIRAL PATH MEANING: *CHALLENGE OF LOYALTY*

The Hound is a fierce challenger, with its loyalty given totally to that which it guards. The Hound challenges you to be trustworthy, loyal and faithful before it will accept you as companion.

Raven

◆

KINGDOM: Strength
TRINE: Challenge
TEACHING: Challenge of Darkness

MYTHOLOGY AND FOLKLORE

In early stories the Raven was often interchangeable with other members of the crow family, notably the crow itself, the chough, the rook and the jackdaw. As carrion birds, Ravens were most of all associated with battle and death and with the deities of war and destruction, yet they were also respected for their cunning, intelligence and 'voice' of prophecy.

Many legends tell that the Raven was originally white or silver in colour, but that it was turned black as punishment for some sin. In one story, the Ravens on Noah's Ark were white but were turned black after feeding on the corpses of the drowned. In Celtic legend, Ravens are generally associated with dark, chthonic forces and death, and in particular with the battle-goddess Morrigan and her sisters Badbh and Nemain, each of whom could take Raven form. Morrigan, as a Raven, would stand on the battlefield and foretell the outcome of the conflict to the Dagda, the All-Father god of the Tuatha de Danaan, the legendary Irish tribe. The Danes also believed that the result of a battle could be discerned by observing the attitudes of Ravens.

The Raven is particularly associated with the Celtic god-king Bran the Blessed, whose name means 'Raven'. After his death, Bran's severed head was carried to the White Mount in London, where it continued to speak prophecy and to protect the island from invasion for many centuries. King Arthur, Bran's descendant, eventually had the head removed as a symbol that he himself had become the land's protector, but today the Tower of London stands on the site of the White Mount, and a long-standing tradition tells that if the tame Ravens kept within the tower should ever leave, Britain will fall. For this reason the birds' wings are kept carefully clipped!

Instances of Ravens involved with prophecy are widespread. It was Ravens who warned the Irish hero Lugh Long-arm of the imminent invasion of the Fomorians, and Ravens reputedly foretold the death of Plato and Tiberius. To see a Raven tapping at the window was a sure sign of death within the household. On a more positive note, young maidens in Orkney and Shetland believed that a Raven seen at Candlemas would indicate by its flight the direction of their ultimate marital home. Several members of the Raven family, including crows and magpies, are the subject of widespread predictive rhymes such as 'One for Sorrow, Two for Joy'.

Ravens appear in a number of Arthurian stories and Grail legends, particularly in the form of 'raven-women' – indeed, Morgan herself once appeared in this form. In the *Mabinogion* story of *The Dream of Rhonabwy*, Arthur's followers attacked an army of Ravens belonging to the hero Owain, while Arthur and Owain played a board game known as *gwyddbwyll* (a similar game played in Ireland was known as *bran-dubh* or 'black raven'). Arthur's forces were getting the better of the encounter until Owain, still playing the game, commanded that his standard be raised on the battlefield, at which the Ravens attacked with renewed vigour and killed many of Arthur's finest warriors. A Cornish legend tells that the soul of King Arthur himself became a chough after his death, and therefore it is extremely bad luck to kill one.

For the Norsemen, especially the Danes, the Raven was an extremely potent war-symbol. During battles they flew their black luck-flag with its Raven emblem, which would have become a hated and feared symbol during the time of Viking harassment and invasion. The god Odin had two Ravens named Hugin ('Thought') and Munin ('Memory'), who would fly around the world observing and reporting back to Odin. For this reason,

Ravens were feared as spies, and no confidences would be spoken within earshot of the birds.

Despite their strong association with death, Ravens also have links with solar deities including Apollo, for whom they were also an important oracular bird. In the Mithraic religion, the first rank of initiation was the Raven, or 'servant of the sun'. Ravens, especially if they have a few white feathers among the black to attenuate the evil, may be regarded as the protector of prophets – it was Ravens who fed Elijah in extremity, and they also came to the aid of Paul the Hermit, St Cuthbert and St Bernard. Ravens may be the supernatural guardians of treasure, or may turn their treacherous nature to good by revealing the hiding places of wrong-doers. They were also popular witch-animals, both as familiars and as shape-changing forms. Some stories tell that Ravens contain the souls of wicked priests.

CHARACTERISTICS: *Foreknowledge; Prophecy; Cunning; Intelligence; Change; Battle; Opportunism; Selfishness; Scavenging; Protection*

In a spread, the Raven represents a sharp, quick intelligence and the talent to anticipate or predict events. It can signify the ability to turn any situation to personal advantage, sometimes without regard for the consequences or for others. It may also suggest a tendency towards dangerous pursuits of various kinds. The Raven has an appetite for the acquisition of knowledge, and knows how to use that knowledge to its own best advantage.

SPIRAL PATH MEANING: *CHALLENGE OF DARKNESS*

The Raven offers the challenge of the unknown. With its prophetic cry muted, it teaches the ability to overcome the dark forces of uncertainty, ignorance and death.

Weasel

◆

KINGDOM: Strength
TRINE: Intelligence
TEACHING: Holder of the
Strength of Mind

MYTHOLOGY AND FOLKLORE

The Weasel has a deserved reputation as an agile, fierce and efficient hunter with excellent hearing and sight. Like the fox, it is credited with intelligence and cunning, and will 'dance' to charm its prey before moving in for the kill. A Weasel will tackle prey many times its own size, and is confident and bold in its dealings with humans, showing little fear. Generally a solitary hunter, the Weasel will occasionally take its young along to teach them hunting skills. Traditionally, the Weasel is the only animal other than the cockerel to be able to kill the fierce basilisk.

Perhaps because of its boldness and daring towards humans, the Weasel was generally regarded in legend as a creature of ill-omen, whose call presaged death and disaster, and whose very appearance on your path brought bad luck. This villainous image has persisted even into modern stories such as *The Wind in the Willows* and *Winnie the Pooh*, where the Weasel is represented as a dangerous and feared criminal.

A white Weasel was feared as a ghost and as a particularly bad portent. Interestingly, though, the Weasel's close relative the stoat – known in its white winter coat as the ermine – was considered a symbol of purity and chastity. If the ermine's coat became soiled, it would die. In many cultures the wearing of ermine fur was reserved for a privileged class, and even today the ceremonial robes of a Peer of the Realm are traditionally trimmed in ermine.

To kill a Weasel, or disturb its nest, was considered extremely bad luck; tradition has it that the Weasel's relatives would take revenge by poisoning the perpetrator's milk, or by following them around for the rest of their lives! Witches were thought to take the form of Weasels to cause mischief and evil.

In Ireland, however, the possession of a purse made from the skin of a piebald Weasel was considered extremely lucky. A Weasel crossing your path, particularly turning to the left, was generally held to be unlucky, but it could also mean that you were going on a voyage. In Wales, a Weasel running ahead of you without turning off could foretell a win.

CHARACTERISTICS: *Boldness; Strength of Mind; Cunning; Charm; Fearlessness; Activity; Privilege; Efficiency; Confidence; Retribution*

In a spread, the Weasel represents the cunning and courage to take on any situation; this boldness, however, may lead to rash actions. It may also signify the importance or need for activity and involvement. The Weasel shows an active curiosity and interest in events and people, which may border on the nosey.

SPIRAL PATH MEANING: *HOLDER OF THE STRENGTH OF MIND*

The Weasel teaches the ability to focus the mind; with courage, this can help you overcome problems and situations which at first seem insurmountable.

Fox

◆

KINGDOM: Strength
TRINE: Intelligence
TEACHING: Mirror of the Mind

MYTHOLOGY AND FOLKLORE

In folklore, the fox is held in particular affection. It enjoys a reputation for charm and humour, perhaps stemming from the expression of its mask, which is frequently perceived to be 'laughing'. Certainly the Fox's reputation for intelligence has basis in fact, as it is adept at avoiding traps and hunters. In most popular stories, the Fox is the epitome of cunning, guile and duplicity; it is admired for its great intelligence, but uses it to deceive for its own ends. In some Christian myths, the Fox is identified with Satan as the Deceiver.

Many stories concerning the Fox's cunning hunting habits are mostly untrue. The Fox will, for example, supposedly run round and round a mesmerized chicken until the bird gets dizzy and falls over, thus becoming easy prey. Alternatively, a Fox will stroll nonchalantly under the branch on which a bird is sitting until, straining to watch the Fox, the bird will over-balance and fall off the branch. Another trick is to bury itself in the earth as though dead in order to leap out and capture the carrion birds who come to feast on its body.

Common belief has it that a Fox with fleas will carry a stick or clump of wool to a river, and then slowly submerge itself until the fleas, to avoid drowning, have nowhere left to go but onto the object. The Fox will then let the object and its passengers float away.

Another symbol of the Fox's duplicity is its reputation for

hunting well away from its own lair in order to lay the blame for any mayhem on other foxes; an old proverb says 'Foxes prey furthest from their earths'. This habit led to the image of the Fox being used in the Middle Ages to satirize itinerant churchmen who had no parish of their own, but travelled the countryside making trouble for resident priests and monks. This in turn led to the popular medieval cycle of stories of 'Renard the Fox', in which the Fox was often depicted wearing monks' clothing as a disguise to keep unsuspecting victims off their guard.

The Fox was a shape-changing form favoured by witches, and its behaviour could also be used as an augury for telling the weather. Any person bitten by a Fox would die seven years later. In Wales, seeing one Fox was considered good luck, but to see more than one was a bad omen. In Scandinavia, the Aurora Borealis was known as 'The Light of the Fox'.

Nevertheless, a Fox's brush was a powerful luck charm, and was used to ward off evil; even today some people use a fox's brush in much the same way as a rabbit's foot. Foxglove flowers, as the name suggests, were thought to have been worn by Fox cubs to keep their paws warm. The bluebell – still called in some places the fox bell – also has a strong association with the animal. The story goes that a Fox, being hunted for its tail, appealed to God for help. God created the pretty blue flower with bells which would ring to warn the Fox of the approach of any hunter.

CHARACTERISTICS: *Cunning; Craft; Slyness; Intelligence; Adaptability; Opportunism; Trickster; Wordly Wisdom; Dynamism; Humour; Competitiveness; Luck*

In a spread, the Fox represents the intelligence and craftiness to take advantage of the world. It may represent adaptability, the ability not to take oneself too seriously, and the capacity to learn from mistakes. The Fox can gain enormous satisfaction from besting others.

SPIRAL PATH MEANING: *MIRROR OF THE MIND*

By meeting your own reflection, the Fox teaches you the ability to laugh at yourself and your mistakes, and to view life with humour and appreciation.

Wren

◆

KINGDOM: Strength

TRINE: Intelligence

TEACHING: Carrier of the Light of
Reason

MYTHOLOGY AND FOLKLORE

The Wren is closely associated with the turning of the seasons, the representation of the Old Year which must be sacrificed to let in the New. As an important kingship symbol, the sacrifice of the Wren provided a substitute for the sacrifice of the king himself to ensure the health and renewal of the land. In Ireland, the Wren was ritually hunted every St Stephen's day and carried in procession by the 'Wren Boys'; and a number of British folk songs also refer to the ritual hunting of the Wren, including the song known as 'The Cutty Wren'.

In Celtic legend, the Wren was one of the birds associated with Bran, the giant king of England who, when mortally injured in battle, requested his head to be cut off and placed at the Tower of London so that it could continue to protect the depleted land. Before its eventual burial there, the severed head continued to speak and give prophecy for a number of years. In another legend, Bran was said to have assumed the shape of a Wren and hidden in an ivy bush to escape pursuit. Perhaps for this reason, the Wren was considered a prophetic bird and was widely used for augury. It was also closely associated with druidic practices.

The Wren was often known as 'the king of the birds', an unlikely title for such a small beast. The story goes that all the birds were gathered to see who would become king, and it was decided that whoever could fly the highest would gain this title. The eagle was confident, and soon flew higher than all his challengers, right to the very limit of his ability. He was just about to return and claim his crown when the tiny Wren, who had been secretly hiding among the feathers on the eagle's back, emerged from its hiding place and flew even higher, thus claiming the prize.

The Wren has a long association with the robin. Sometimes the Wren represents the archetypal female and the robin the male; at other times the Wren represents the Old Year and the robin the New. In either case, there are many references to battles between them and to one bird slaying the other. The familiar nursery rhyme 'Who Killed Cock Robin', although in its modern form an 18th-century political rhyme about the British Prime Minister Robert Walpole, is probably an echo of an older story of the battle between the robin and the Wren.

Another old story tells how the robin and the Wren were both part of the relay of birds that brought a burning brand from the sun to present the gift of fire to humankind. The Wren was the first bird in the chain and had to snatch the fire from the sun itself, as a result of which all its feathers were burned off. In gratitude for their tiny colleague's bravery, all the other birds – except the owl, which refused – each donated one feather to restore the Wren's plumage. For this reason, the Wren appears to be an untidy and scruffy bird with feathers of many different colours and patterns. Nevertheless, keeping Wrens' feathers was once held to be a potent protection against drowning.

A common belief in earlier times was that Wrens roosted in caves, hence their Latin name *Troglodytes troglodytes*, which means 'cave dweller'. In fact Wrens may take advantage of natural or artificial roosting places, including caves, especially in the winter when large numbers may roost together for warmth and protection. In the summer, however, the birds will build large, round nests, which may also have influenced their solar symbolism.

CHARACTERISTICS: *Bright Intellect; Busyness; Ambition; Clear Thinking; Intellectual Pursuits; Forward Planning; Acceptance of Change; Turning of the Years; Perception; Prophecy; Sacrifice*

In a spread, the Wren represents the end of one cycle and the beginning of a new one, or the death of old ideas and values and the intellectual stimulation of new challenges. It can also mean the ambition to help others, but with an in-built need for recognition and status. The Wren has the ability to release the past, leaving itself untethered to take on each new cycle in its life.

SPIRAL PATH MEANING: *CARRIER OF THE LIGHT OF REASON*

The Wren offers the bright light of intellect and reasoning to see beyond the near horizon and to balance the darkness of the soul.

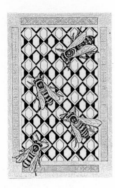

Bee

◆

KINGDOM: Strength

TRINE: Creation

TEACHING: Creator of Order

MYTHOLOGY AND FOLKLORE

Bees have been widely respected throughout many cultures. Even today, the more traditional apiarists tell of the importance of being polite to the hive, and of telling the Bees of great events such as a marriage or, more particularly, a death in the family. Bees indeed have great associations with death and with the soul, and are often seen carved on tombstones. They may presage death if they swarm on a dead tree or on a house, and should never be moved without first explaining the reasons to them.

Credited with great wisdom and understanding, Bees are thought to have foreknowledge of major events as well as stores of old knowledge and lore – a Scottish saying goes 'ask the wild Bee for what the Druids knew'. Tradition has it that Bees should never be bartered or sold, but the gift of a hive will bring good luck to both donor and recipient.

Although Bees have some sexual associations – with their ravishing of the flowers for their nectar and their phallic sting – they have also been associated with chastity and purity. The Romans believed that bee-keepers had to remain sexually chaste, and a long-held tradition claimed that swarming Bees would not sting a girl passing through them if she were a virgin.

Early Roman myths associate the Bee with the Great Mother, and it was also held in esteem by the Mithraic religion, in which it was regarded as a representation of the soul. An early belief was that Bees were born from the dead bodies of animals, particularly the lion and the ox; this symbolism occurs in the Old Testament story of Samson, among other places. In Brittany, it was believed that the Bee had its origin in the tears of Christ at the Crucifixion. Another Christian tale holds that Bees were the only animal to come unchanged from Paradise, and therefore they are known as 'the little servants of God'.

Bees are symbolic of productive hard work, and were used as a model for early monastic settlements, not just in the shape of the 'beehive' buildings, but in the orderly running of the tasks of the community. The fruit of the Bees' labour – honey – was the most widespread sweetener before the introduction of sugar, and mead or honey-wine was also much sought. Beeswax was used for candles, and the sting was – and indeed still is – used as a cure for rheumatism and neuritis.

CHARACTERISTICS: *Creation of Order; Communications; Knowledge of Events; Wisdom; Understanding; Creativity; Organizational and Management Skills; Productive Labour; Sexuality; Activity*

In a spread, the Bee represents hard work which will eventually prove fruitful. It can mean the ability to communicate ideas, and the need to be kept informed of events. The Bee is able to create order and to organize skills and people, whether in the running of a business or a home. The Bee may also represent understanding and pure intent.

SPIRAL PATH MEANING: *CREATOR OF ORDER*

The Bee's hive is the order of the universe. Inside, the Bee teaches you your own place within this order, and the order within your own life.

Horse

◆

KINGDOM: Strength
TRINE: Creation
TEACHING: Bridge between
the Worlds

MYTHOLOGY AND FOLKLORE

Since earliest times, the Horse – provider of power and transport
– has enjoyed perhaps the closest relationship with humans of
all the animals. The Horse has been identified with deities of both
sun and moon, but was perhaps most closely associated with the
land itself, its health and its cycles. Horses represent strength,
swiftness, beauty, sexual vigour and fertility – extremely desirable
attributes for early cultures.

Horse symbolism appears in the earliest known paintings, as
well as in some major landscape art forms, such as the giant white
Horse carved into the hillside by the settlers at Uffington in
Berkshire. Much archaeological evidence exists of the importance
of a sacrificial Horse in early ritual, and the kingship ceremonies
of ancient Ireland involved the use and sacrifice of a white mare
as a symbol of the kingdom. Even today, the people of Britain
observe a strong taboo on the eating of Horse flesh, which dates
from these earliest times.

Epona (sometimes known as Rhiannon) was the Celtic Horse
goddess, whose name has given us the modern word 'pony'. She
is usually depicted riding a mare and followed by foals. Epona's
Irish counterpart was known as Macha, an Otherworld woman
who, when heavily pregnant, was forced into a foot race against
a Horse. Macha won the race but, on passing the finishing line,
gave birth to twins and then died, first placing a curse on the king
of Ulster who had forced her into the race. The curse ensured that

in times of greatest danger all the warriors of Ulster would become 'as weak as a woman in childbirth'. The ancient capital of the kings of Ulster was named 'Emain Macha' after her, and its remains can still be seen in County Antrim.

The Saxon invaders who supplanted the Celts in much of the east of Britain also held the Horse in great reverence, and their battle pennants were typically made from the tails of white Horses. The white Horse is still a common theme in arms and symbols from areas of the country with strong Saxon influences, for example appearing on the arms of the county of Kent. To the Saxons, eating horse flesh was taboo, but this would be broken in a special horse-feast held in October.

People who worked with Horses accrued great respect; this included riders, charioteers and the smiths who shod the Horses. The legend of the 'smiths' word' persisted until very recent times. Passed from father to son it would immediately cause even the wildest beast to become docile and compliant if whispered into a Horse's ear. The Saxon god known as Volund, or Wayland, was a smith-god. In Berkshire, there is the ancient burial mound known as 'Wayland's Smithy' where, if a Horse were left tethered overnight under a full moon, the owner would find it the next morning magically and expertly shod.

Magical Horses were the means by which mortals could travel between the worlds – a method also used in many shamanic traditions. The Celtic sun god, Lugh, is quoted as being the first to introduce horsemanship into Ireland, but the most famous Horse in Irish myth is Aonbharr, the mount of the sea-god Manannan, who made any rider invulnerable. She carried away the hero Conan to the Celtic Otherworld, from where he had to be rescued. Later heroes have also travelled between the worlds in this way, including the well-known 'Thomas the Rhymer' who was taken to the land of faerie mounted on the milk-white steed of the Elf Queen, and Tam Lin who escaped from the fairy realm on a stolen white Horse.

There are also many legends associating Horses with the sea and its gods. Tales of mortals being carried into the sea to 'drown' often represented a dangerous journey into the Otherworld from which there may be no return. The Manx 'glashtin' were water-horses – identical to ordinary Horses except that their hooves were back-to-front – who would trick mortals into mounting their backs, then dash back to their home in the sea, drowning the riders. Other water-horses would emerge from lakes and rivers at night to feed on the corn in surrounding fields, and again if mounted they would carry off the rider to their own realm. White-tipped waves breaking against the shore are even now referred to as 'white Horses'.

In Norse mythology, the god Odin possessed a magical, eight-legged stallion named Sleipnir, who could outrun every other Horse and could run across water as though it were dry land. On the death of Baldur, the much loved and revered god of light, it was Sleipnir who carried Odin's son Hermod to the Norse Underworld to beg the goddess Hel for his return.

In medieval times, much supernatural activity was associated with the Horse, with countless tales of ghostly, often headless, steeds careering around the countryside. Horses that had been bedded down for the night, rested and well-fed would be found in the morning exhausted and wild-eyed having been used by witches for various nefarious purposes; these mounts were said to have been 'hag-ridden'. At night, the master of the Wild Hunt would lead his pack of hounds through the sky mounted on a wild black stallion; in the morning, the marks of the Horse's hooves could often be discerned on rooftops. King Arthur's own Horse, shod in silver, can reputedly still be seen on certain nights galloping around Cadbury Hill in Somerset.

Many towns and villages held festivals at the turning of the seasons which featured a 'hobby Horse' being ritually led through the streets amid much singing and dancing. These ceremonies contained echoes of earlier beliefs in which the Corn Spirit or Earth Goddess took the form of a Horse at harvest time, and the hobby Horse may represent a substitute sacrifice for renewal of the land. A few of these ceremonies still survive in places – the hobby Horse ceremony in Padstow, Cornwall, for example, held on May Day.

Because of their importance, much effort was expended in

protecting Horses from evil influences. Horse brasses were affixed to the harness as charms; it was important that these were kept well-polished, as the reflected light would frighten away the evil spirits. Such Horse 'charms' have been found in even the earliest Celtic burial places. Horses' tails were plaited to ward off witches.

The horseshoe is well known as a potent good-luck symbol. Forged in fire from the magical element of iron and shaped to resemble the horns of the new moon, it brings protection on a house if hung over the doorway. With the 'horns' of the shoe pointing upwards, the horseshoe represents luck; with the horns pointing down, protection. To find a horseshoe in the road is considered extremely lucky, and no marriage ceremony is complete without a horseshoe symbol to wish the couple well in their life together.

CHARACTERISTICS: *Emotions: Creativity; Harvest; Healing; Sexuality; Friendship; Practicality; Hard Work; Physical Pleasures; Caring; Assuredness; Emotional Strength; Communication*

In a spread, the Horse represents the ability to work well with others and to help carry other people's burdens. It may also signify the strength of friendship, and the fortitude to reach out to others to create compromise and understanding. The Horse is very sociable, but although it may be hard-working and practical, it also has a wild side to its nature.

SPIRAL PATH MEANING: *BRIDGE BETWEEN THE WORLDS*

The Horse creates a bridge between awareness of the Outer World and of the Inner World, offering guidance and companionship on your journey between them.

Spider

◆

KINGDOM: Strength

TRINE: Creation

TEACHING: Spinner of Life

MYTHOLOGY AND FOLKLORE

The Spider was regarded as the ultimate spinner and weaver, two tasks that formed a vital part of the economy in early societies, and which were extended to become an allegory for the patterns of life itself. The Spider was associated with all goddesses of spinning and weaving, and with the Great Goddess archetype, representing the universal Mother and Weaver of Fate. The symbol of the supernatural female spinner whose work dictated the destinies of mankind for good or ill was an extremely widespread and well-understood allegory, and the Spider represented the natural symbol for this concept. Some traditions also hold that the Spider's web represents the 'lost' thirteenth sign of the zodiac, again indicating a strong link with fate and destiny.

The Greeks believed that the Fate Clotho spun the thread of life, and wove it into the patterns of destiny. The goddess Athene, who was patroness of spinning and weaving, was challenged to a contest by the human woman Arachne. When Arachne beat her, Athene, in a jealous rage, transformed the girl into a Spider, condemned to produce thread from her body through all eternity.

In Welsh myth, the spinner and weaver is Arianrhod, sister of the magician Gwydion and mother of the hero Llew. Arianrhod is the mistress of the Otherworld tower of initiation, Caer Sidi, whose shape reflects the spiralling thread. Arianrhod's spinning wheel is the wheel of stars, and her threads those of life, creation, birth and rebirth.

An early Christian legend tells how when Herod's soldiers were searching for the infant Jesus, a Spider hid the baby by spinning a concealing web across the place where the family were hiding. In recognition of this service, the common garden Spider carries the distinctive mark of the cross upon its back. In more recent folklore, Spiders were considered a good omen, and it was extremely unlucky to kill one, particularly in the house. A country tradition holds that if you find a 'money spider', you should pick it up by the thread and circle it around your head three times to bring good luck in money matters. To see a Spider actually spinning its web would mean that new clothes were about to be acquired. Spiders and their webs were important ingredients in many medieval cures and remedies, especially for gout, ague and whooping cough. It was considered a particularly lucky omen if a Spider dropped from the ceiling onto a person's face!

The patience and determination attributed to the Spider are perhaps best represented in the apocryphal story of the Scottish king, Robert the Bruce, who, on suffering defeat in battle, was hiding from his enemies in a cave. Downhearted by his defeat, he was inspired by the persistence of the Spider sharing his hideaway who, no matter how many times her web was broken, would patiently start again at the beginning and persevere until the task was completed. Seeing this as a reflection of his own situation, Robert the Bruce went out and rebuilt his army to continue the struggle against the English.

CHARACTERISTICS: *Destiny; Patterns of Life; Fate; Creation; Craftsmanship; Birth; Life Goals; Agility; Persistence; Patience; Guardianship; Parenthood*

In a spread, the Spider represents creativity at all levels: the creation of arts and crafts, of new paths and patterns in life, or of new life itself through children. It may represent the ability to know the best time to start, maintain or end particular parts of your life, or may signify a feeling for purpose or destiny. The Spider is in charge of its own life, creating its own patterns and paths.

SPIRAL PATH MEANING: *SPINNER OF LIFE*

The Spider teaches the interconnectedness of all things. It shows you the web that radiates from your own life, enabling you to feel all the forces that touch it.

Lion

◆

Spirit of the Kingdom
of Strength

TEACHING: The Sovereignty of Strength

MYTHOLOGY AND FOLKLORE

The Lion appears in *Beasts of Albion* as a mythic beast. Although tales of real Lions may well have been brought back to Britain by traders or, later, by soldier crusaders, the animal would have been regarded by the ordinary people of the islands in much the same way as the unicorn or the dragon.

The symbol of the Lion became extremely important, representing sovereignty and valour, and the Lion was eventually adopted as the principal heraldic beast of both England and Scotland. The solar symbol of the Lion is frequently seen as locked in conflict with the lunar unicorn, with the Lion emerging triumphant, and this theme appears from early Greek coins to Lewis Carroll's *Alice* stories. In some tales, the unicorn represents the spring and the Lion summer; in other versions, the Lion is day and the unicorn night. An early rhyme, repeated by Carroll, tells:

The Lion and the Unicorn were fighting for the crown:
The Lion beat the Unicorn all round the town.
Some gave them white bread, some gave them brown:
Some gave them plum cake and drummed them out of town.

The inclusion of both animals as supporters on the armorial bearings of the Royal coat of arms dates back to the reign of King James I of England.(who was also James VI of Scotland), who included the unicorn as a symbol of his Scottish kingship and the

Lion as a representation of the English throne. The rhyme quoted above probably first became popular during the Jacobite wars as an allegory of the struggle between England and Scotland; it is likely that Carroll was using the beasts as a political metaphor for Gladstone and Disraeli.

A number of stories tell how, in gratitude for help and compassion, a Lion may become the faithful companion and battle-helpmate of a warrior or hero. The most familiar story is probably that of Androcles, who compassionately removed a thorn from a lion's paw, only to have the lion rescue him in turn. But the theme can also be found in the Arthürian story of Owain who rescued a Lion beset by serpents, and in the stories attached to Sir Bevis of Hamtun, who was befriended by two Lions while in the Holy Land. A depiction of Sir Bevis's Lions can still be seen guarding the medieval Bargate in Southampton. In both cases, the Lions travelled with the heroes and rescued them from danger.

The Romans used the image of the devouring Lion in funerary art as a symbol of death, with depictions of the hunting and slaying of the Lion representing triumph over death. In the Old Testament, the Lion is a common symbol of strength, especially controlled or restrained strength. It is also an emblem of St Mark as a sign of divine royalty. The image of the devouring Lion is also used in Christian iconography as a symbol of the triumph of Satan; perhaps a throwback to the stories of early Christians being given to the Lions in the Roman arena.

Popular myth attributed a number of curious habits to the Lion. It was believed that the beast slept with its eyes open, and so representations of guardian Lions adorned entrances and doorways, especially to churches and sanctuaries. Guardian Lions are still widely used in monuments and statues to this day, perhaps the best known being those at the base of Nelson's Column in Trafalgar Square, London. Lion cubs were reputedly born dead, and remained in that state for three days, guarded by the lioness, until their sire arrived to breathe life into them, a resurrection myth exploited by the medieval church. Like bears, Lions were reputed to mate only once every seven years, but would then create such a furore that cattle and livestock for miles around would be terrified. The Lion was also reputed to wipe out the trace of its track with its tail as it walked.

Widely regarded as the king of the beasts, the Lion is a symbol of dauntless courage and bravery – 'lionheart' being a particularly flattering epithet for a warrior. The Lion is a common heraldic beast in the devices of Royal dynasties and aspirants. The golden Lion was an early symbol of English kingship, with the red Lion representing Scotland and silver Lions adopted by the native princes of north and south Wales. The Lion may be depicted in heraldry in a number of different attitudes, and is often shown holding swords, lances or even heads between its paws. Variants include the marine Lion, representing maritime power, and the dragon-lion, which incorporates some of the symbolism owned by the Dragon. In the nineteenth century, the Lion was used in political satire as a representation of the power of Great Britain, where it could be seen in company with the Russian Bear, the French Cockerel and the American Eagle, to name but a few.

As a symbol of both spiritual and temporal power, C.S. Lewis made use of the Lion imagery for 'Aslan', his representation of the Christ figure in the popular chronicles of Narnia. It is interesting to note that Lewis's God-Lion exhibits the classic characteristics of power, guardianship, companionship and sacrifice, and even echoes the earlier folklore by using his breath to awaken life.

CHARACTERISTICS: *Strength; Bravery; Maturity; Responsibility; Victory; Nobility; Reason; Guardianship; Leadership; Growth; Challenge; Intelligence; Creation*

In a spread, the Lion represents the maturity and nobility to use strength in a measured and controlled way. It can also signify a victory over adversity, or the courage to make sacrifices for the benefit of others. The Lion uses his strengths to provide leadership, protection and companionship.

SPIRAL PATH MEANING: *THE SOVEREIGNTY OF STRENGTH*

As the Spirit of the Kingdom of Strength, the Lion teaches that strength can be a beautiful and merciful power. The Lion is powerful, yet gentle, and is a king, companion and servant to his people.

Bear

◆

KINGDOM: Wisdom
TRINE: Awakening
TEACHING: Guide to Dreams

MYTHOLOGY AND FOLKLORE

Bears are no longer found in Britain, having died out in the late Middle Ages, but their strength, power and ferocity ensure that they are an abiding symbol. Surprisingly few images or stories featuring Bears have been found in Celtic, Saxon and Norse myth; yet early portraits and carvings feature the beasts, and there is much evidence of their skins being highly prized as warm clothing and coverings. The associations that do remain are generally with hunter gods and goddesses, and in the company of other wild emblems such as the boar and the stag.

Graeco-Roman myth tells how the infant Zeus was hidden and looked after by two Bears, who later became the constellations Ursa Major and Ursa Minor. These star groups are almost universally associated with the Bear image. Bears were sacred to the goddesses Artemis and Diana, and in the cult of Artemis young girls were dressed in yellow robes and called 'Bears' before being allowed to marry.

In Roman society, Bears were familiar participants in the arena, either as performing pets, as executioners for criminals, or in the 'sport' of bear-baiting, where a Bear would be encouraged to fight a number of trained dogs. It is likely that these entertainments were brought to Britain by the Roman invaders, and bear-baiting remained popular until medieval times.

The Celts had two goddesses who took the form of the Bear, Andarta and Artio, both of whose names contain elements of the

Celtic word for the Bear, 'Artos' or 'Arth', echoes of which can still be found in a number of place names. There is some evidence to suggest that King Arthur also derived his name from this root – the constellation of the Great Bear is known in Wales as 'Arthur's Wain'. The legend of Arthur sleeping in an underground cavern awaiting the day of his awakening is also reminiscent of the Bear's hibernation. Bears appear to have both solar and lunar attributes; he-bears represented masculine traits and were sacred to Thor; and she-bears were associated with feminine moon-goddesses. The Celtic lord of the animals, Cernunnos, is depicted on the Gundestrop cauldron accompanied by a Bear and other wild animals.

The Bear's hibernatory habits, and the fact that the new-born young emerge after the winter sleep already mobile and active, have led the animal to be associated with rebirth and renewal. One belief was that the cubs were born underground as shapeless lumps which the mother Bear would then 'lick into shape' before they could emerge into the world. Another belief was that Bears would mate only every seven years, but that when they did they set about with such vigour that they would cause disturbances in the air sufficient to cause miscarriage in cattle.

In a common form of the English medieval mummers' play the Bear was cast as the villain, terrorizing a flock of sheep represented by small boys before being put to flight by the hero-shepherd. Generally, the Bear seems to have been respected for its great strength, but with the knowledge that, with caution, the strength could be contained and harnessed. 'Tame' Bears performing tricks and dances were a common sight in medieval times. It was believed that the eye of a Bear placed in a beehive would make the bees prosper, and that riding on a Bear's back would cure a child of whooping cough – both examples of how a Bear's power may be harnessed for good.

Nowadays, the most familiar image of the Bear is probably that of the cuddly 'teddy bear', or of cute and fluffy animals in television cartoons. This modern sanitization has undermined the traditional power and potential ferocity of the beast, and has completed the weakening of the archetype which began with the use of performing Bears.

CHARACTERISTICS: *Introspection; Contained Strength and Power; Protectiveness; Deliberacy; Patience; World of Dreams; Potentials*

In a spread, the Bear represents the emergence of abilities and potentials which have lain dormant. It can signify a down-to-earth approach to life, but with an awareness of the Inner World; or it may represent waiting for the right time for something to happen. The Bear is slow to rouse, but can be extremely fierce when provoked.

SPIRAL PATH MEANING: *GUIDE TO DREAMS*

The Bear lies deep within the earth. It awakens the understanding of dreams and potentials within yourself.

Cockerel

◆

KINGDOM: Wisdom

TRINE: Awakening

TEACHING: Herald of Awakening

MYTHOLOGY AND FOLKLORE

Although a comparative late-comer to the islands of Britain – chickens were unknown until introduced by the Romans – the Cockerel quickly established itself within the mythology and folklore of the land. Its penetrating early-morning call to greet the sunrise would be the first sound many people heard each day, and would indicate the end of darkness and the start of the day's work.

The Romans held the Cockerel sacred to Mercury – the herald of the gods – and he is often depicted accompanied by the bird. The cult of Mithras also featured the Cockerel as a symbol of the sun god. The reverence for the bird seems to have been quickly adopted by the native Celts, and Julius Caesar remarked that Britons would not eat the flesh of hares, geese or chickens, holding them to be sacred. Cockerels were adopted into the Celtic cults of Mercury, the goddess Brigid, and the Mother Goddess, and a native goddess is depicted accompanied by the bird on an altar at Corstopitum.

Norse mythology tells of two Cockerels: the golden Vithafmir, standing in the sun at the crown of Yggdrasil, the tree of life, guards against evil; while the red Cock Fralar lives in the Underworld and will wake the heroes for the last great battle. This symbol of awakening is repeated in Christian tradition, where it is held that all the Cocks in the world – including those on the top of church spires – will crow to herald the Resurrection and Armageddon.

The Cockerel has, in fact, a particularly prominent place in Christian stories. A Cock crow heralded the birth of Jesus, while the crowing of the Cock confirmed the accuracy of the prediction of Peter's denial. The Cock guards against evil, yet a black Cockerel could be seen as a creature of the devil and of black magic.

A common sacrificial animal, the Cock was a traditional offering to the goddess, Brigid – later amalgamated into the Christian St Brigit – on 1st February at the feast of Imbolc. Live Cockerels were buried at the meeting of three streams for good fortune, and were commonly incorporated into the foundations and doorways of new buildings to protect them against misfortune.

As a bird of the sun, the Cockerel was thought to be a particularly effective protection against ghosts, spirits and other creatures of the night. The Cockerel was not just a passive guardian, being well-known for its ferocity when roused, and was associated with a number of gods of war. Cock-fights, in which two aggressive Cockerels, sometimes armed with vicious artificial spurs to complement their own natural weapons, were pitted against each other for sport were common throughout the Middle Ages and indeed, sadly, still occur illegally today. Along with the weasel, the Cock was held to be the only animal that could successfully kill the evil and magical basilisk.

The Cockerel was also seen as a representation of the Corn Spirit. In many areas the bird's shape was a popular form of the 'corn dolly', made by weaving the last corn stalks of the harvest into shape. These 'corn Cocks' were placed as protection on top of the ricks at harvest time.

CHARACTERISTICS: *Boldness; Cockiness; Self-confidence; New Beginnings; Vocation; Awakening; Realization; Bluster; Heralding; Guardianship; Communication*

In a spread, the Cockerel represents the confidence to turn your back on old fears, and to start a new way of life – but beware of over-confidence. It can also represent an awakening to a new realization, an enthusiastic embracing of change which may lead to a new direction or vocation. The light heralded by the Cockerel banishes doubt and uncertainty.

SPIRAL PATH MEANING: *HERALD OF AWAKENING*

The Cockerel tells of the awakening of the Inner Self, the inspired light rising from the inner darkness. In its highest form, the Cockerel is the voice of prophecy.

Bat

◆

KINGDOM: Wisdom

TRINE: Awakening

TEACHING: Guide through Darkness

MYTHOLOGY AND FOLKLORE

Because of its nocturnal habits and the fact that it lives in dark, hidden places like caves and woods, the Bat has generally been associated with the powers of darkness and the night. Its unusual physical characteristics made it difficult to categorize, with early people uncertain whether to treat it as a bird or as a flying rodent. Because of this uncertainty, the Bat inspired a fear of the unknown, and was a particularly potent omen in Medieval times.

Bats were among those animals most closely associated with witchcraft, and the form of a Bat was thought to be particularly favoured as a shape-change. Bats also featured in many spells and recipes – Shakespeare has his witches in *Macbeth* including 'wing of bat' in their brew. A Bat flying near a person or, even worse, into the house, was regarded as a sure sign that someone was attempting harm with a witching spell; a Bat flying three times around the house was a sign of imminent death in the household. In Scotland, the belief was held that if Bats flew swiftly upwards and then quickly descended to earth again, it was a sign of the 'witching hour' when the forces of darkness had power over all humans.

Medieval Christian belief confirmed the Bat's dark image, associating it with the forces of evil and representing it as a manifestation of Satan, who is frequently depicted with Bat's wings. The Bat was also sometimes seen as a symbol of loneliness and unhappiness, as it abides in ruined and empty places.

Conversely, it was believed in some parts that to keep a Bat's bone about the person would ensure good luck; one superstition even tells that to keep a Bat's eye in the pocket would render a person invisible.

One widespread belief concerning the Bat, persisting even today, is that if the creature should fly into a woman's hair, it will become entangled and may only be freed by cutting the hair. This rumour has no basis in fact, and indeed was disproved by the Earl of Cranbrook in 1959 who, with the help of three volunteers, attempted the feat with three different kinds of Bat, each of which easily freed itself from the hair and flew away. Nevertheless, many people will still throw their arms protectively around their head whenever a Bat flies near them.

The Bat's highly developed 'sonar' sensing system ensures that it will rarely fly into any obstacle by mistake, and it is able to manoeuvre skilfully at high speeds to detect and catch its insect prey. Many of the Bats found in Britain are sociable animals, and live in colonies for mutual benefit and protection, forming 'nurseries' to rear their young. Bats are relatively long-lived, and have few enemies but man. They are able, when not active in hunting food, to lower their body temperatures and enter a state approaching torpor, which conserves energy.

The abiding image of the Bat in the 19th and 20th centuries, however, is probably that of the vampire: the 'undead' shape-changer which needs a constant supply of human blood to survive, and which by taking blood from its victims spreads and reproduces its own kind. The vague whisps of legend from central Europe were widely promulgated following Bram Stoker's novel *Dracula* and, more importantly, through the avid interest of Hollywood. The vampire, with its underlying sexual imagery, and themes of resurrection and good versus evil, has now become an archetype in its own right, but one which is nevertheless valid in that it includes many of the themes, plots and messages inherent in the earliest stories.

Some salvaging of the Bat's image has also emerged in the 20th century with the widespread popularity of the comic-book hero 'Batman'. This caped crusader fights crime and evil, but retains an air of mystery and hidden secrets and uses his exploits to counter his own melancholy and tragedy. It is also interesting to notice how Batman's associate 'Robin', retains many of the traditional characteristics of the Redbreast: companionship, daring, loyalty and compassion (see page 104).

CHARACTERISTICS: *Hidden Fears; Guidance; The Subconscious; Mental Fears and Horrors; Sexuality; Introspection; Psychic Powers; Inner Strengths; Direction*

In a spread, the Bat represents the ability to overcome the horrors and restrictions created by the mind. It can also represent deep, hidden fears which you are reluctant to bring into the light of examination. The Bat is able to act as a guide for others because of its ability to see through the darkness and fears, and to avoid hidden obstacles.

SPIRAL PATH MEANING: *GUIDE THROUGH DARKNESS*

The Bat is your guide to flying beyond the restrictions and fears of the intellect and the self.

Bull

◆

KINGDOM: Wisdom
TRINE: Empowering
TEACHING: Power of Stability

MYTHOLOGY AND FOLKLORE

The Bull is an extremely powerful early symbol of strength, fertility and ferocity, and has been both venerated and sacrificed for many thousands of years. Some of the earliest paintings and sculptures from Britain depict Bulls, and they are generally closely associated with kingship, the fertility of the land, and the sun. Bulls were usually sacrificed at the height of their strength and prowess, and the blood from the beast was allowed to soak into the earth to imbue it with fertility.

The Celts associated the Bull with the god Beli, the great father of all life, and also with the horned god Cernunnos. Many relics have been found of triple-horned Bulls, associating this animal with the magical number three (making it also a particularly potent symbol in *Beasts of Albion*). Sculptures have also been found of the Bull with three cranes and, at Maiden Castle in Dorset, with three goddess figures on its back.

The Druidic ritual of cutting the sacred mistletoe with a golden sickle was followed by the sacrifice of two white Bulls. In Ireland, when the time came to choose a new High King, a druid would engage in the ritual of 'Tarbhfhess', which involved eating the flesh and drinking the blood of a slaughtered Bull before sleeping wrapped in its flayed hide. Thus prepared, the druid would dream of the man who was the rightful king.

Herds of cattle, and at the centre a powerful and virile Bull, were a vital part of early Irish economy, culture and society. Cattle were used for ploughing, pulling and meat, as well as for milk products, and form a pivotal part in much of the early folklore. The well-known Ulster epic of the *Tain Bo Cuailnge* ('the cattle-raid of Cooley') emphasizes this point.

King Ailill and Queen Maeve were joint rulers of the kingdom of Connacht, and were held to be equal in every way. On comparing their possessions, however, it was found that Ailill owned the fabulous white Bull FInndbennach, for which Maeve had no match. Enraged, Queen Maeve set about scouring Ireland for an equivalent beast, until she heard of the brown Bull, the Donn of Ulster, which appeared to be every bit as powerful and virile as the white Bull. Connacht and Ulster fought a great war – in which the hero CuChulainn, among others, was killed – for possession of the Donn, and it was eventually captured and taken to Connacht in triumph. However, the brown Bull and the white Bull were both too proud to share the same pasture, and they eventually fought each other to the death. Both Bulls in this story were said to have been born in supernatural ways. Their original incarnations had been as two magical swineherds who engaged in a shape-changing battle, and who had finally metamorphosed into Bulls after having been ravens, water monsters, human warriors and eels.

The epic struggle between the god Mithras and a Bull lay at the heart of the Mithraic religion, which at one time seriously challenged Christianity within the Roman Empire, being particularly popular among the Roman military. Mithras, born from solid rock, was forced to fight and slay a magical Bull, the first living creature created by the God of Light. Mithras did not wish to kill the magnificent beast, and turned his head away as the knife plunged down. Where the rivers of blood from the Bull fell upon the earth, however, grass, flowers and corn grew up in great abundance. The Bull was the great Creator, whose sacrifice and death was necessary to create life.

Mithras is often depicted as riding on or slaying the Bull, and initiates into the cult underwent the ceremony of the Taurobolium, in which they were baptized in Bull's blood, emerging to a new life. The remains of several temples to Mithras can still be seen in Britain, including a well-preserved shrine in the City of London, in Queen Victoria Street, between Mansion House and St Paul's Cathedral. A story from Hyssington in Montgomeryshire recounts how the vicar of the local church fought an epic battle against a giant Bull which shrank in size as long as the priest prayed and read the Bible at it. Whenever the priest stopped, the Bull started growing again. This is probably an allusion to the battle between the church and the challenge of the Mithraic cult.

Thunder gods, including Zeus and Jupiter, were associated with the Bull, whose bellow sounds like the roar of thunder. These gods were also linked with oak trees; a number of very old trees in England – including one in Windsor Forest – were known as 'Bull oaks' and were associated with hauntings and with supernatural activity.

Ceremonies and children's games involving invocation of the Bull persisted throughout the Middle Ages. Bull masks were used in parades and ceremonies on festive days. The custom of Bull-running, in which a fierce Bull was let loose in the streets, is recorded in Stamford in Lincolnshire; a similar tradition still survives in Pamplona, Italy. Horn fairs and ceremonies associated with Bulls are also recorded in Dorset and Hampshire. Echoes of Bull-worship and sacrifice can still be found in some of the traditional songs and rhymes linked to horn fairs.

Bull-baiting was widespread until at least 1835. Carried out before slaughter, this practice ostensibly improved the flavour of the meat. Children played a game known as 'Bull in the barn', which involved forming a ring around a designated 'Bull' who would then attempt to break out by sheer force.

CHARACTERISTICS: *Strength; Virility; Fertility; Stability; Steadfastness; Vigour; Determination; Potency; Sacrifice; Maturity; Courage; Ferocity; Destruction; Forces of Nature*

In a spread, the Bull represents a steadfast determination to achieve a goal, although this may be perceived as stubbornness or the inability to accept new ideas. It can also signify a raw energy for living life to the full, which may become destructive if unstable or uncontrolled. The Bull has a strong, well-developed personality which matures into a stable, well-balanced attitude towards life.

SPIRAL PATH MEANING: *POWER OF STABILITY*

The Bull offers the power of stability, the strength of foundation upon which all things can be built; it is the centre of the wheel of the seasons.

Brock

◆

KINGDOM: Wisdom
TRINE: Empowering
TEACHING: Holder of Tradition

MYTHOLOGY AND FOLKLORE

The Brock, or badger – despite long-standing and continuing ill-treatment by humans – is generally regarded in folklore to be a steady, tenacious and home-loving beast, but one possessed of enormous courage and power when angered or driven to extreme measures.

Many products taken from the Brock were considered lucky or beneficial. In Scotland, the sporran – the purse worn with traditional Highland dress – is made from Brock skin, and Brock grease was, until comparatively recent times, sought as a curative for many ills. Brock hair – put in a black cat-skin bag and tied around the neck when the moon is fewer than seven days' old – was said to ward off witchcraft. The tooth of a Brock, kept about the person of a gambler, was said to ensure the winning of any wager.

The Brock is a creature of almost unbreakable habit, keeping rigidly to established paths and tracks used for many generations even in the face of modern-day obstacles such as roads and housing estates. An extremely sociable beast living in extended family 'tribes', the Brock is generally shy of human company, being active mostly at night and during the warmer months. Although it does not actually hibernate, the Brock spends most of the winter underground.

The Brock is an extremely powerful creature who will use its massive strength to remove any obstacles from its established paths. It can also fight ferociously when cornered, as evidenced by the distasteful and now illegal 'sport' of badger-baiting where single badgers are often pitted in uneven contests against a number of dogs.

An ancient game, called 'badger in the bag', involving 'running the gauntlet' between two lines of boys armed with sticks, is believed to have originated from the *Mabinogion* story of Gwawl and Rhiannon. Rhiannon was promised in marriage, against her will, to Gwawl, but chose instead to wed the Welsh hero Pwyll. Gwawl appeared as a stranger at the wedding feast, and Pwyll rashly agreed to give him whatever he most desired. Gwawl immediately demanded both the feast and Rhiannon. Pwyll was forced to agree, but in turn attended the wedding feast for Gwawl and Rhiannon in a disguise of his own, and carrying a sack which he requested be filled with food. When Gwawl attempted to comply with this request, it became apparent that the sack was magical, and that no amount of food would fill it. Pwyll claimed that the sack could only be filled if a nobleman were to press the food down with his feet. Gwawl complied and stepped into the sack, whereupon Pwyll pulled it up over his head and tied it at the neck. As each of his retainers came to the feast, they hit the bag with a stick and asked 'What have we in the sack?', to which the others replied 'A badger!'

CHARACTERISTICS: *Security; Home-loving; Family; Sociability; Tradition; Comfort-loving; Cautious; Gentle; Slow to Adapt; Reliable; Determined; Tenacious; Predictable; Powerful when Threatened; Habit; Single-mindedness*

In a spread, the Brock represents a love of peace, security, the home and family. It can symbolize reliability, but with a tendency towards staying on the safe path, and showing an inability or unwillingness to be adaptable or adventurous. The Brock has the strength and determination to overcome any obstacles placed in the way of achieving a goal, and can be powerful and fierce when threatened.

SPIRAL PATH MEANING: *HOLDER OF TRADITION*

The Brock offers the power of tradition, the strength and support of the accumulated wisdom of previous generations, enabling the guided growth of awareness and understanding.

Stag

◆

KINGDOM: Wisdom

TRINE: Empowering

TEACHING: Power of Choice

MYTHOLOGY AND FOLKLORE

In early stories, the appearance of the Stag normally signified a great change in the lives of the participants. The Stag – particularly if it was white – could also be used as a guide into the Otherworld, and as a symbol of the beginning of a series of challenges to be overcome. A symbol of leadership and of light, its death or sacrifice was used to indicate the end of one cycle and the start of a new one.

This symbolism is evident in the story of Pwyll and Arawn, taken from the *Mabinogion*. Pwyll, Lord of Dyfed, was out hunting when he spied a pack of white hounds with red ears – a sure sign of Otherworld origin – pursuing and bringing down a white Stag in the forest. So impressed was he by the magnificence of the Stag that Pwyll beat off the hounds and claimed the body of their quarry as his own. This act incurred the wrath of the owner of the pack of hounds, who turned out to be none other than Arawn, lord of Annwn, the Celtic Otherworld. In compensation for his bad manners, Pwyll was obliged to change places with Arawn for a period of one year, and to fight on his behalf against an Otherworld foe.

In Arthurian legend, King Arthur and his knights would periodically take part in the ritual hunt of a white Stag, the head of which would traditionally be presented to the fairest maiden in the land. At Gwenhwyfar's insistence, the head was presented to the Lady Enid, who had been championed by the Knight

Gereint. Gereint and Enid were married, and after a series of adventures during which Enid's devotion for her husband was returned with indifference and mistreatment, they eventually found true love together.

Stags' horns have also formed part of the attributes of many early deities and power figures. The Celtic god Cernunnos is identified as a Stag-god and lord of the animals. Other images of antlered figures can be found in cave paintings at Trois-Frères, Ariège, France, and on the famous Gundestrop Cauldron.

Later legends feature Herne the Hunter, who may well be an echo of Cernunnos. Herne is particularly identified with Windsor Great Park in Buckinghamshire, and there is even a reference to Herne in Shakespeare's *Merry Wives of Windsor*. In some stories, the antlered Herne is the leader of the Wild Hunt. Between them, Herne and Cernunnos have left a legacy in the many British place names beginning with 'Cern' or 'Hern', and in the once-widespread horn fairs which used to be held in towns and villages to mark the turning of the seasons. The horn fair at Abbots Bromley in Staffordshire still features deer's antlers.

As a solar symbol, the Stag is depicted in conflict with the powers of darkness, often represented by the snake or serpent. Some legends held that the Stag would draw the serpent out of the ground using its nostrils, and would then either devour it or trample it to death, a familiar Christian icon of good over evil. In Norse myth, the Tree of Life Yggdrasil was home to four Stags, who symbolized the four winds.

Its power and agility, and keen senses of smell and hearing ensured that the Stag was a popular and challenging quarry in the hunt, and its potential ferocity when cornered added extra excitement. The beast's strong body allowed it the choice of flight or fight, and the skilled hunter would need to know the animal's habits well to anticipate which choice it would make. The hunting of the Stag was often reserved for kings or great warriors. This tradition was perpetuated in law for many hundreds of years, and formed a prominent feature of the 'Robin Hood' stories in medieval times. Several packs of Stag hounds are still used for hunting the animal in Britain today.

The Stag's ferocious and effective antlers are mostly used during the rutting season, to challenge an existing leader who has his pick of the females, or to defend against the challenge from a would-be usurper. Stags can be extremely aggressive and fierce at this time, and are nervous of confrontation from any quarter. The image of the young Stag challenging the authority of the old leader may be a familiar archetype even today in family situations with growing sons challenging the authority of a father-figure.

An early concept was that of the 'King Stag', leader and protector of the herd, who would be ritually hunted and killed each year to ensure the successful turning of the seasons and the return of summer. Merlin himself, as told in the *Vita Merlini*, once took up the role of 'Lord of the Animals' and, wearing Stags' horns upon his head, led a herd of deer and she-goats.

CHARACTERISTICS: *Strength to Run or Fight; Choice; Avoidance; Responsibility; Protection; Leadership; Rhythms of the Seasons; Sacrifice; Determination; Challenge; Aggression; Self-contained*

In a spread, the Stag represents the choice of whether to fight or flee from a situation. It can mean the possession of the strength to fight when cornered, and the strength to sacrifice yourself for others, or old ideas for new. The Stag prefers to avoid confrontation, however, and often needs to be forced to stand firm rather than running away from events.

SPIRAL PATH MEANING: *POWER OF CHOICE*

The Stag offers you choice and free will; the choice of whether or not to take on responsibility for your life and the consequences for others of your actions or inactions.

Hedgehog

KINGDOM: Wisdom

TRINE: Protection

TEACHING: Shield of the Soul

MYTHOLOGY AND FOLKLORE

The Hedgehog, or 'urchin', is widely regarded as a weather augury. After its winter hibernation, the Hedgehog supposedly emerges on Candlemas day (1st February) to survey the weather. If it then decides to return to hibernation, at least another six weeks of bad weather are due. The belief that the Hedgehog builds its nest with the entrance and exit holes facing away from the prevailing winds was mentioned by Pliny, and carried right through to the 18th century, from whence we get the following rhyme in *Poor Robin's Almanac*:

> Observe which way the hedgehog builds her nest
> To front the south or north, or east or west;
> For if 'tis true that common people say,
> The wind will blow quite contrary way.

Hedgehogs have traditionally been used in cures and remedies, especially for colic, boils and baldness. They were also used to treat leprosy, a disease to which only they and humans are susceptible. The Romanies, who regarded the Hedgehog as a delicacy when rolled in clay and baked slowly over a fire to remove the prickles, also used the animal as a cure for eye complaints. Hedgehogs were reputed to be immune from snake bites – although their prickly skins would probably be an adequate protection – and Hedgehogs have been known to kill and eat snakes. A comb made from the prickly skin of the

Hedgehog could be used very effectively to card wool.

The Hedgehog's agility, good memory for places, acute hearing – which can pick up even the sound of a worm moving underground – and solid defensive spines have allowed it to adapt readily to modern life, despite the heavy toll taken by roads and motorways. Its strategy of curling into a ball thus presenting a solid wall of spines to any attacker is very effective, although some stories hold that the wily fox will tip the Hedgehog into a stream or pond in order to make it unroll. Lewis Carroll made good use of this image in *Alice's Adventures in Wonderland,* where rolled Hedgehogs provide the croquet balls in Alice's match with the Queen of Hearts. The Hedgehog is also reputed to have another use for its spines – rolling onto rotten and softened apples and other fruit in order to spear the food on its prickles and carry it off to the nest.

Despite the affection of many modern families who delight in leaving food for half-tame Hedgehogs in return for watching their noisy eating and playful antics, the Hedgehog has generally been regarded as an ill-omened beast which should be killed to avoid misfortune striking. This bad reputation probably stems from the animal's strong medieval association with witches, who were supposed to take the form of Hedgehogs in order to suck dry the cows of neighbouring farmers. This widely held belief may have some basis in truth, as although Hedgehogs' mouths are too small to suckle from a cow's udder properly, they do enjoy the taste of milk and may lick drips from the teat of a cow ready for milking. The Hedgehog also plays host to numerous fleas, which live on its body from birth to death, a fact that may also have contributed to the animal's poor reputation.

CHARACTERISTICS: *Adaptability; Self-protection; Mischief; Defensiveness; Sensitivity to natural rhythms*

In a spread, the Hedgehog represents a defensive attitude, building a barrier to protect sensitive inner feelings. This may be interpreted by others as aggression or aloofness. The Hedgehog's confidence in its protective coating may tempt it into mischief-making without fear of retribution.

SPIRAL PATH MEANING: *SHIELD OF THE SOUL*

The Hedgehog shields the soul, protecting it with an impenetrable barrier. It teaches that, regardless of the destructive experiences of life which can break down or damage the personality, the soul can always endure as a strong source of knowledge, love and inner strength.

Goose

◆

KINGDOM: Wisdom
TRINE: Protection
TEACHING: The Guardian

MYTHOLOGY AND FOLKLORE

Geese were very familiar to the Romans, who kept them as 'watchdogs' to protect farms, buildings and temples; their noisy alarms at the approach of any strangers giving ample warning of danger. It is said that the citizens of Rome were alerted to the invasion of the Gallic hordes by the noisy warnings of their Geese.

The Celts also held the Goose in great reverence. It is one of the three beasts that Julius Caesar reports were taboo flesh for the Britons of the time. Geese are often depicted in the company of war-gods, and remains of Geese have been found in the graves of warriors. In particular, the Celtic form of the Roman god Mars is often depicted with Geese, both in his aspect of a war-god and as a healer, in which aspect the Geese represented guardianship against disease. Images of Geese were frequently carved above the lintels of doorways to offer protection against unwanted intrusion and illness.

The Celtic horse goddess, Epona, has been depicted riding on a flying Goose, as has Brigantia, the Celtic Great Mother – this is possibly the origin of 'Mother Goose' in nursery rhyme and pantomime. As a symbol of wealth and indolence, owning the 'Goose that lays the golden egg' has also passed into pantomime and popular culture. In medieval times, witches were purported to be carried to their secret Sabbats on the backs of Geese.

In the Middle Ages, Goose was a traditional festive fare at Michaelmas (29th September) and Christmas, and a number of

'Goose fairs' were established around the country to which the birds would be marched. It was traditional in some places for a tenant to give his landlord a Goose at Michaelmas, and may have replaced an earlier tradition of sacrifice. An old rhyme holds that

> Whosoever eats goose on Michaelmas Day
> Shall never lack money his debts to pay.

The view of the Goose as a comparatively stupid animal ('silly as a Goose') is a fairly recent development; earlier cultures recognized the Goose as intelligent and selective. The Goose's stiff-legged walk reinforces the association with military matters in later years, resembling as it did the 'Goose-step' march of trained soldiers. The Roundhead soldiers of the English Civil War were particularly identified with this step, and many familiar nursery rhymes, such as 'Goosey Goosey Gander', stem from this period as a satire on the excesses of the soldiery.

CHARACTERISTICS: *Protection; Aggression; Activity; Belligerence; Territoriality; Wealth; Intelligence; Selectivity*

In a spread, the Goose represents the willingness to protect what you feel is right, and to stand and fight for your ideals. It can also mean that territory is important to you; this could be your personal space in the workplace or at home, or your cherished ideals or beliefs. Any unwelcome intrusion is greeted with alarm and belligerence.

SPIRAL PATH MEANING: *THE GUARDIAN*

The Goose is the guardian of light and truth, balance and harmony, and of right or just causes. An active guardian, it teaches the skills needed to champion the light.

Crane

◆

KINGDOM: Wisdom

TRINE: Protection

TEACHING: Sentry of the
Inner World

MYTHOLOGY AND FOLKLORE

No longer found within Britain, the Crane has long been a symbol of patience and vigilance, guardianship and teaching. Greek and Roman legend depicted the Crane as an ever-vigilant sentry, standing on one leg and holding a stone in the other foot. If the Crane were to fall asleep, the stone would drop and wake him. This watchful symbol was carried through to many medieval heraldic devices.

The Crane also has a strong transformative tradition. Women, especially ill-tempered ones or those convicted of promiscuous sexual behaviour, have customarily been given the form of Cranes as punishment, and this may account for the bird's reputation for ill-omen in some quarters.

Celtic lore contains a number of legends of women turned into Crane form. When still a child the hero Fionn was rescued from falling over a cliff by his grandmother, who transformed herself into a Crane to swoop down and pluck him to safety. St Columba reputedly changed a queen and her handmaiden into Cranes as a punishment. The god Manannan possessed a magical bag made from the skin of a Crane. The unfortunate bird had formerly been a woman named Aoife, who was transformed into a Crane because of her jealousy. This bag was used to hold a number of magical items which were only visible at high tide, and which were handed down to a number of gods and heroes in Irish legend. These items formed the main treasures of the island.

The Crane is a symbol of the solar god Apollo, but is also associated with a number of war-gods. For a warrior to see a Crane on the way to battle was an extremely bad omen, possibly due to the legend of the Irish god Midhir, who had three Cranes as guards. These Cranes had the ability to rob warriors of their courage and fighting ability.

The Crane was also associated with death. In Welsh legend, the Crane is a form taken by Pwyll, Lord of the Underworld, and Irish stories tell of the four Cranes of Death who are the enchanted sons of an old woman, the 'Hag of the Temple'. Flying Cranes may also represent the released souls of the dead, or the death of the old year. In Greece the Crane Dance was used to mark the start of the New Year. A number of important Celtic artefacts depict the Crane associated with the bull, and with the cutting of a willow tree. This may also be a representation of the turning of the year.

The flight of Cranes was studied carefully, both as an oracle and weather augury and for instruction and example. The Cranes' habit of flying in a triangular formation with the strongest birds leading and protecting and the weak and young guarded in the centre was taken as a symbol of good government and responsible society. It is said that Mercury invented the alphabet from studying the patterns of Cranes' flight. The three-toed, branching shape of the Crane's foot was seen by some as a representation of the family tree, and led to the English word 'pedigree' which is *pied de grue* – Crane's foot.

Both the stork and the heron shared much of the symbolism of the Crane. All three can be found in mythology and heraldry in very similar roles, combining flight and solar attributes with water and feminine roles. Of the three, only the heron is still found commonly in Britain.

CHARACTERISTICS: *Protection; Vigilance; Patience; Transformation; Inner World; Poise; Calm; Stillness; Jealousy; Promiscuity; Concentration; Female Strengths; Guardianship; Self-control*

In a spread, the Crane represents the need to be patient and to find inner stillness in the rush of everyday life. It may signify the necessity for control of a potentially excessive temperament, and may also indicate the hiding of feelings or true potentials from other people. Although the Crane appears calm and still, it is constantly vigilant and alert to all that happens.

SPIRAL PATH MEANING: *SENTRY OF THE INNER WORLD*

The Crane guards the doorway between Outer World behaviour, problems and reactions, and the Inner World treasures of stillness, timelessness and calm.

Owl

◆

KINGDOM: Wisdom
TRINE: Knowledge
TEACHING: The Catalyst of Self

MYTHOLOGY AND FOLKLORE

Today the Owl is probably most closely associated with wisdom – the 'wise old Owl'. Some modern archetypes have taken this one step further to make the Owl a rather more ridiculous figure who *thinks* he knows everything, but is in fact rather foolish. Through most of the early folklore, however, the Owl has been regarded as a bird of ill-omen.

In Britain the call of the Owl was widely believed to signify death, particularly if it was heard during the daytime, for three nights running, or if the bird was seen to sit and cry on the roof of a house. Worst of all, an Owl coming into the house or down the chimney was a sure sign of impending death within. Shakespeare, in *Macbeth*, refers to the Owl as 'the fatal bellman which gives the stern'st good night', and cites owlet's wing as an important ingredient 'for a charm of powerful trouble'. An Owl hooting at the birth of a child signifies an unhappy life, and even seeing an Owl in the daytime may bring bad luck. In Wales, there is a legend that the sound of an Owl calling signifies that an unmarried maiden has just lost her virginity.

The Owl has been associated with a number of legendary female figures. Through its link with the Greek goddess Athene (and the Roman and Celtic equivalents, Minerva and Sulis), the Owl acquired its reputation for wisdom, as Athene was regarded as patroness of the arts and of prudent intelligence. An even earlier association is made in Hebrew legend between the screech-owl and Lilith, who was reputed to be Adam's first wife, created at the same time as Adam and who fell from grace to become the first of Satan's four wives. In Scotland, the Owl is known as *cailleach* or 'old woman', and is linked to the Cailleach Bheur, the blue-faced crone figure who represents the season of winter and death.

In Celtic legend, the Owl appears in the story of Llew in the *Mabinogion*. Llew was put under a curse by his mother Arianhrod, which meant that he could never marry a mortal woman. Llew's uncles, the magicians Math and Gwydion, created a magical bride for Llew from flowers of oak, broom and meadowsweet, and named her Blodeuwedd, that is 'face of flowers'. Unfortunately, the newly created Blodeuwedd remained faithful to Llew 'for only as long as flowers keep their fragrance', and she fell in love with a passing hunter named Gronw Pebr, with whom she plotted Llew's death. They nearly succeeded but Llew was found grievously wounded in the form of an eagle by Gwydion and nursed back to health. In punishment for her betrayal, Gwydion turned Blodeuwedd into an Owl, and since that time her name has been the Welsh word for an Owl.

In the Celtic legend of the 'Quest for Olwen', the Owl appears as one of the five oldest beasts on the earth, the others being the blackbird, the stag, the eagle and the salmon. This longevity also reinforces the association of the bird with old knowledge.

Charms and remedies made from parts of the Owl could be used to cure many ills, especially those of the mind or the eyes. Eating raw Owl's eggs supposedly cured habitual drunkards of all desire for strong drink, and eating the salted meat of the bird was a remedy for gout brought on by over-indulgence.

CHARACTERISTICS: *Self-realization; Self-knowledge; Analysis; Determination; Wisdom; Transition; Clear-sightedness; Forced . Adaptability; Awareness; Ruthlessness; Patience; Intellect*

In a spread, the Owl represents the death of the old order; its call warns that you must be prepared to adapt to a new way of thinking, to accept the loss of the old and familiar. It can also represent the ability to see clearly through the darkness of chaos, confusion and deception, and the need for self-examination. The Owl may have a tendency for over-analysis or criticism.

SPIRAL PATH MEANING: *THE CATALYST OF SELF*

The Owl forces self-transformation and realization, bringing the dark wisdom of the subconscious into the light. It brings death to the old self, and challenges you to understand who you are and to achieve your full potential through self-examination.

Cat

MYTHOLOGY AND FOLKLORE

Nowadays we have accepted the Cat into our lives and homes and see it as a loving, if somewhat independent, companion. Some surviving superstitions concerning Cats, however, remind us that the Cat was long regarded as a sinister, powerful animal associated with the dark moon, and considered the familiar of witches or the embodiment of evil fairies. It was also attributed with predictive and psychic powers.

The Celts had stories of monster Cats which ravaged the countryside. Perhaps the most powerful was Cath Palug, who was born in Anglesey to the magical sow Henwen. Henwen's alert swineherd, Coll, recognized the danger of Cath Palug as soon as he was born, and immediately threw him into the sea from the top of a high cliff. Instead of drowning, however, the kitten struck out for the far coast, and set about his career of destruction. Some time later, King Arthur and his kinsman Cei undertook a special hunting expedition to Anglesey to slay the beast. (French variants of this legend, in which the Cat is known as Capalu, have the monster killing King Arthur in France before invading England and being crowned king.)

Another story tells how St Brendan, the famous Irish explorer, was forced by a storm to take refuge on a tiny island. No sooner had he landed, however, than a wild-eyed man came running towards him, warning him to put out to sea to avoid a terrible monster. As soon as Brendan set sail again, a monster Cat came bounding towards him and started swimming hard towards the boat. Only the fervent prayers of the saint and his crew saved them, with another Cat of even greater size rising from the deeps to engage their attacker.

The Cat's nocturnal habits, large litters and finely tuned hunting skills are responsible for some of its associations. In Scandinavian mythology, the Cat was connected with Freyja, a moon-goddess of passion and fertility, whose chariot was pulled by giant Cats. In Ireland, Cats were regarded as cruel, evil fairies.

The Cat possessed great psychic and divinatory power, and people who knew how to take advantage of this power could make use of it for their own ends. In Ireland, the eating of Cat flesh formed a part of the prophetic ritual known as Imbis Forosnai. In the Highlands of Scotland, legend told of the powerful king of the Cats who could answer any question. The only way that humans could force it to do so was by slowly roasting another feline over a fire. Attracted by the animal's suffering, and to save it more pain, the king would appear and do the summoner's bidding. Scottish legend also tells of the Cait Sith, the fairy Cat with dark-green eyes and extremely long ears.

The belief in divinatory powers of Cats persisted into medieval times, when they were supposedly able to see spirits and to predict death or disaster. Cats, like rats, would leave a building or ship before its destruction, and they were therefore considered very lucky to keep on board ship or in mines; sailors and miners would not, however, risk losing the luck by mentioning the word 'cat'. A Cat deserting a sick person was a sure sign that the patient would die, and to drive a Cat away was considered unlucky. In the English fens, a Cat who slept upstairs was a warning of imminent flooding – a widespread danger in that area. The power of the Cat could be harnessed as a protection for a new building by walling-up a still-living Cat into part of the structure; the mummified bodies of animals used for this purpose are still found during restoration work on medieval buildings.

Perhaps the most well-known and widespread aspect of the Cat was its association with witches, either as a vessel for a witch's familiar demon, or as a favoured shape-changing role for the witch herself. In some areas, people would not talk openly if there were a Cat present, in the belief that the beast would turn back into human shape and spread any intimate secrets it might have overheard.

A Cat should never be left by a sleeping baby, as it would sit on the child and suck its breath away. Kittens born in May were particularly unlucky, and were reputed to bring adders into the house; and those born just after Michaelmas (when the Devil was believed to be abroad in the world) were known as 'Blackberry Cats' and could be expected to be particularly mischievous.

Even today, echoes of the earlier superstitions are still fairly widespread. Black Cats crossing the path are still thought to be unlucky (or lucky, depending on which part of the country you are in). Cats' remarkable capacity for self-preservation has resulted in the widespread tale of them having 'nine lives', and early associations of Cats used as weather predictors have given us the phrase 'raining cats and dogs'. A well-known superstition is that when selecting a new kitten from a litter, the Cat should be allowed to choose its owner, rather than the owner selecting the Cat.

CHARACTERISTICS: *Secrets; Intuition; Psychic Ability; Luck; Independence; Patience; Individuality; Self-Contained; Grace; Instinct; Dignity; Heightened Awareness; Hidden Knowledge; Sensuality; Curiosity; Aloofness; Neurosis*

In a spread, the Cat represents patience and determination to achieve personal goals, although there may be a tendency to act impulsively without thinking through the consequences. It can also represent the holding back of some secret, hidden part of your nature, or a sensitivity to the moon and tides. The Cat meets the world on its own terms, and demands respect and consideration without necessarily offering anything in return, maintaining an aloof, self-confident image.

SPIRAL PATH MEANING: *HOLDER OF HIDDEN KNOWLEDGE*

The Cat holds the hidden knowledge of the rhythms of nature, the moon, the tides, Fate, the spirit world and the sub-conscious. Its knowledge is not given freely or easily, but must be earned.

Salmon

◆

KINGDOM: Wisdom
TRINE: Knowledge
TEACHING: Keeper of Ancestral
Knowledge

MYTHOLOGY AND FOLKLORE

Regarded as an ancient and powerful store of wisdom and knowledge, the Salmon was greatly respected, particularly by the Celts. Its natural habits would certainly reinforce this respect, as the Salmon can live in both salt and fresh water, and performs prodigious feats of stamina and perseverance in returning upstream to its spawning grounds against all obstacles. One of the amazing feats of which the Irish hero CuChulainn was said to be capable was the 'Salmon Leap', which enabled him to clear tall obstacles and walls. Even today, fish are associated with the mind and powers of wisdom, and eating fish is said to be 'good for the brain'.

The Salmon was particularly associated with deep pools and wells, especially those sheltered by hazel trees, as feeding on hazelnuts gave the Salmon its great wisdom. Each nut consumed would cause another red spot to appear on the Salmon's back, and would increase its wisdom. Anyone who could catch the Salmon and eat its flesh would acquire the stored wisdom. Guardian Salmon, however, when removed from their pools and killed, would often miraculously revive from the frying pan and make their way back to the pool, either in their own form or by taking human shape.

Perhaps the best known Celtic Salmon was Fintan, the famous 'Salmon of Knowledge'. Fintan was reputed to have originally been a mortal, a survivor of the Great Flood, who hid in a cave in the form of a Salmon for many centuries, gaining knowledge of all that happened in Ireland. The great druid Finegas hunted this Salmon by the banks of the River Boyne for seven years, meaning to devour it to gain the knowledge for himself. Finegas had as his pupil the young Fionn mac Cumhal, later to be one of Ireland's greatest heroes. Finegas eventually managed to catch the Salmon, and set it to cook on a spit over a fire watched over by the young Fionn, who had orders not to touch the fish. In turning the Salmon on its spit, however, Fionn burned his thumb on the hot flesh, and instinctively put his thumb in his mouth to cool it. Immediately, all the acquired wisdom of the Salmon was gained by Fionn, and for ever afterwards he need only place his thumb in his mouth to have foreknowledge of events.

The supposed great longevity of the Salmon also features in the Welsh story of Culhwch and Olwen. One of Culhwch's heroic tasks in his quest for the hand of the daughter of the giant Yspaddaden was to find the god Mabon, who had been imprisoned. Culhwch enlisted the help of a number of animals and birds, each older than the last, and each of whom passed the hero on to a new guide. The final and oldest beast was the Salmon of Llyn LLyw, who knew the place where Mabon was kept. This story demonstrates, once again, the link between great age and knowledge.

The Salmon was a favoured shape-changing form of many great Celtic magicians, particularly in ritual sequences or battles. The bard Taliesin took the form of a Salmon in his battle with Ceridwen; and Tuan Mac Carill, the last survivor of the original invaders of Ireland, became a Salmon as the last in a series of transformative beasts. Like Fintan, he was reputed to have lived for many centuries and to know the entire history of Ireland. Tuan Mac Carill was finally captured and eaten in the form of a Salmon by the wife of the king of Ireland, after which he was reborn once again in human form.

In Norse myth, the Salmon was the form chosen by the god Loki when fleeing the wrath of his fellow gods after the death of Baldur. Loki's cunning and ingenuity led him to invent the first ever fishing net, but this caused his downfall as Thor and the other gods used his own invention to chase him through the pool in which he was hiding. In desperation, Loki leapt high over the net, but Thor caught him in his hands. The Salmon attempted to escape, with its slippery scales sliding through Thor's fingers, but Thor grasped the tail and he and the other gods bound Loki to a rock to await the coming of Ragnarok. Loki's tormented writhing is said to be the cause of earthquakes.

CHARACTERISTICS: *Ancestral Knowledge; Culture; Memory; Story Telling; Perseverance; Determination; Endurance; Single-mindedness; Adventure; Transformation*

In a spread, the Salmon can represent the stamina to battle against adverse forces blocking your path in life. It can also represent the acquisition of knowledge, and the need to express and use it in everyday life. The Salmon takes on seemingly impossible challenges, but its strength and determination often enable it to succeed where others have failed.

SPIRAL PATH MEANING: *KEEPER OF ANCESTRAL KNOWLEDGE*

The Salmon holds the wisdom of all those who have lived on the land since time began; it offers awareness of their blood in your veins, and of forgotten knowledge.

Dragon

Dragon

Spirit of the Kingdom
of Wisdom
TEACHING: The Wisdom of Kings

MYTHOLOGY AND FOLKLORE

Perhaps the most widespread and abiding mythological animal symbol, occurring across a wide range of cultures, races and eras, is that of the Dragon. Also referred to as the worm or serpent in some stories, the Dragon is a fundamental symbol of supreme power, both the elemental power of primal, natural forces, and more secular, temporal power. It has been used on the standards and emblems of warriors, kings and emperors through the centuries. The Celts used the Dragon banner as a symbol of kingship; the Romans as an emblem for the formidable military unit, the cohort; the Vikings raided the coast in Dragon-prowed longboats; the Saxon royal standard was adorned with the emblem of the white Dragon; English kings from Richard I to Edward IV fought under its likeness. Even today, the red Dragon of Cadwallader, once the badge of King Arthur, is the well-recognized emblem of Wales.

Descriptions of Dragons generally agree on a number of major points: they are usually huge in size, although in Wales they are thought of as less terrifying, bird-like creatures; their bodies are reptilian and scaled, with long, sinuous tails; and their mouths breathe fire or poisonous fumes. Many Dragons are associated with watery places, and they are usually regarded as good swimmers. Some Dragons may fly, although others – especially if they are known as 'worms' or 'serpents' – may have only vestigial wings, or none at all.

According to Geoffrey of Monmouth, 12th-century bishop and chronicler, a flaming, dragon-shaped comet appeared to King Uther, the sire of King Arthur, to signify his forthcoming conquests against his enemies; thereafter Uther adopted the golden Dragon as his battle-standard and was known as 'Pendragon'. This term appears to have been a badge of war-office or leadership, as *The Anglo-Saxon Chronicles* report tales of Cerdic's victory over 'Naud and his Pendragon'.

In Arthurian legend, the young Merlin was summoned to the court of the Welsh king Vortigern, who had been attempting to build a mighty tower, which kept falling down. Vortigern's magicians had decreed that the tower's foundations should be strengthened by the sacrifice of a fatherless child, and Merlin had been brought for this reason. Merlin's prophetic powers, however, revealed a hidden pool under the foundations of the tower which, when drained, exposed two battling Dragons, one red and one white. After an intense period of fighting, the white Dragon overcame the red. This vision pointed not only to the ascendancy of the white Dragon of the Saxons over the red of the Celts, but also the chaos and ruin of the land when no strong ruler wields power.

In Norse myth, the serpent Jormungand, offspring of the god Loki, encircles the whole world and bites its own tail. The Dragon Nidhogg lies at the foot of the world tree Yggdrasil, gnawing at the roots and devouring corpses. The Anglo-Saxon emblem of the Dragon is found in a number of written sources and on surviving artefacts. A particularly fine shield decoration from the Sutton Hoo ship burial depicts a stylized Dragon, and in the eighth-century epic poem *Beowulf*, the hero meets and conquers a water Dragon at great personal cost. The Norman invaders also used the symbol, and there is a Dragon depicted on the Bayeux Tapestry.

In Scotland and the north of England, there are numerous local tales of monstrous 'worms', their activities in many cases accounting for particular features such as hills or chasms. These huge worms had scales and sinuous tails, but unlike 'true' Dragons could not fly, although many were associated with water and could swim. The Stoorworm was particularly enormous. It caused great destruction and could only be restrained by the sacrifice of a maiden. The hero Assipattle killed the beast by lighting a fire in its liver, and its death throes formed the islands of Orkney, Shetland, Faroe and Iceland, and the Skaggerak channel. The Lambton Worm from Derbyshire could rejoin its body parts if cut in two – a fairly common facility of Dragons. Near the Uffington White Horse in Wiltshire is Dragon's Hill, where St George reputedly killed the Dragon, and the top of the hill is bare to this day where the poisonous blood flowed.

Dragons generally fall into one of three categories. Hoarding Dragons do little harm to humankind, and indeed have very little interaction with people. They hide in the dark, secret places of the earth with their treasure hoard, and dream. Dragons slain by heroes or saints are generally not regarded as guardians of treasure, as the worth of the hero would be diminished by the material gain. These beasts are symbols of the elemental forces, or of heathen practices to be overcome by the champion of right and light. The third type of Dragon is the destructive, ravaging beast which eats livestock and humans and brings misery to the countryside. These beasts are often associated with water or bottomless wells, and may forbid access to a river, well or other water source – as such they too may be thought of as guardians of the treasures of the Underworld. Dragons are generally regarded as intelligent, wise and cunning adversaries; the Dragon Fafnir, slain by the hero Sigurd, was said to be a wise and magical creature whose flesh would give the power to communicate with the birds and the beasts.

The medieval church used the symbol of the Dragon as a metaphor for paganism and non-Christian belief; the motif of a Christian knight or saint slaying the Dragon represented the victory of Christianity over paganism. Satan himself is depicted in Dragon form being cast out from Heaven by the Archangel Michael. Among more than 40 Dragon-slaying saints of the early Western church, St Michael and St George are particularly well-recognized in Britain; the story of George, a Roman saint, was brought to Britain during the time of the crusades, and he supplanted the English king Edward the Confessor as patron saint of England. Many churches dedicated to St Michael and St George were built on the sites of important centres for earlier religions. St Patrick's casting out of the serpents in Ireland also represents the victory of the early church there.

The metaphor of the Christian knight slaying the Dragon was extremely widespread in medieval pageants and mummers' plays. These often featured complex Dragon costumes operated by several men, with jaws that could open and shut to frighten the spectators. Dragons were also used in religious plays and iconography as representations of the Devil.

The symbol of the Dragon is still popular today in literature, television and film. Tolkien's 'Smaug' in *The Hobbit* was a wise and wily guardian Dragon, but also ravaged the countryside when roused. His slaying, in traditional manner, led to kingship for the champion Bard. Anne McCaffrey's 'Dragon' books have moved the creatures to a new world and made them wise companions, but still the representatives of power and leadership. Dragons feature frequently in children's cartoons as fearsome adversaries for the hero to overcome.

CHARACTERISTICS: *Strength of Personality; Independence; Self-reliance; Shrewd Intellect; Determination; Achievement; Solitude; Luxury; Wealth; Earth Power; Leadership; Judgment; Life Force; Vitality; Awakening; Empowering; Protection; Knowledge*

In a spread, the Dragon represents inner knowledge and the need to search for this treasure. It can symbolize the strength to be independent and self-contained, and a love of luxury or wealth, or it may signify the destructive misuse of knowledge. The Dragon, although strong, often takes too much on itself, and sees turning to others for help as a weakness.

SPIRAL PATH MEANING: *THE WISDOM OF KINGS*

As the Spirit of the Kingdom of Wisdom, the Dragon teaches the beauty of the power of knowledge, the responsibility for wisdom and judgment in the use of knowledge, and the disaster and destruction its misuse may bring.

Dolphin

◆

KINGDOM: Purity
TRINE: Compassion
TEACHING: Guide to Tears

MYTHOLOGY AND FOLKLORE

For centuries Dolphins and porpoises have been greatly respected by seafarers. There are numerous stories, from the earliest legend to the present day, of drowning sailors being guided to shore by a Dolphin. Ulysses' son Telemachus was saved in this way, according to Homer, and ever afterwards the Greek hero carried the symbol of the Dolphin on his shield. Some legends tell of Dolphins being originally human, which accounts for their friendship and affinity with humankind.

Roman art contains many examples of Dolphin images, including some especially fine mosaic floors, some of which still exist in Britain. The image was particularly prevalent in funerary art, as the Romans believed that Dolphins accompanied human souls to paradise. The Celts seem to have had similar beliefs. They also associated the Dolphin with female divinities and mother-goddess figures and, possibly, with the rebirth of the soul after death. As a maritime symbol, the Dolphin had particular importance for the island race of Britons. Images of gods and mortals riding on the backs of Dolphins can be found in several early artefacts from around Europe, one good example being on the famous Gundestrop Cauldron.

As its reputation for helping sailors would suggest, the Dolphin was regarded as a good omen by most seafarers, and to harm or kill one was extremely unlucky. One travelling alongside the ship at the beginning of a voyage brought immense good luck. Dolphins were said to have detailed knowledge of the winds – some stories held that they actually controlled them. The sight of Dolphins leaping out of the water would presage a storm, but seen on the surface when a storm was already raging, they would indicate calm weather to come shortly.

The strong link between human and Dolphin continues today, despite the ill-treatment of the beast in some parts of the world. Dolphins' intelligence and learning capacity are well-recognized, and their curiosity and friendliness towards boats and people make them welcome and familiar companions. Many people who have swum alongside Dolphins, either wild or captive, can testify to their sense of fun and play, and interaction with the beast is becoming widely accepted as a therapy for a number of nervous and mental disorders. The symbol of the Dolphin has been adopted as an emblem by environmental groups, and is now widely recognized as a representation of an intelligent and caring approach to the environment.

CHARACTERISTICS: *Empathy; Sensitivity; Compassion; Intelligence; Playfulness; Joy; Gregariousness; Helpfulness; Communication; Intuition; Emotions; Openness*

In a spread, the Dolphin represents emotional sensitivity and a deep feeling for people, although this may manifest in 'wearing the heart on the sleeve'. It can also symbolize the ability to listen to and act on inner-feelings, or it may signify the importance of interaction with others and the self-fulfilment this can bring. The Dolphin has a love of life and cares deeply about people, other animals and the environment.

SPIRAL PATH MEANING: *GUIDE TO TEARS*

The Dolphin guides you through the surface emotions down into the deeper levels of the self. It teaches expression of the emotions of the spirit, in joy and compassion for the world around you.

Wolf

---♦---

KINGDOM: Purity
TRINE: Compassion
TEACHING: The Mentor

MYTHOLOGY AND FOLKLORE

The Wolf was the longest-surviving large predator in Britain. Although the last specimens in England and Wales probably died out in the late 15th century, they survived in remote areas in Ireland and Scotland until as recently as the early 18th century.

The Wolf still evokes conflicting emotions. Many fairy tales cast it in the role of villain, from the frightening images in the story of Red Riding Hood and the Three Little Pigs to the modern terror of Hollywood's werewolves. There are still echoes in some stories, however, of the Wolf's earlier role of teacher, nurturer and companion – even the Big Bad Wolf is an intelligent beast, versed in riddles, whose task within the tale is to bring out a moral lesson.

Rudyard Kipling's teacher-wolf role model is familiar to modern generations both through two *Jungle Books* and for its adoption by the scouting movement. This archetype has very early origins. The fact that Wolves live and operate in efficient packs which depend on co-operation and mutual dependency may explain why the teaching element was considered important. Although they can be fierce and ruthlessly efficient in the hunt, attacks on humans were always rare.

Wolves were credited with great wisdom, which could be shared with mortals under certain circumstances. The druid Bobaran, on meeting the white Wolf of Emhain Abhlac, undertook a particular ritual to acquire for himself the beast's insight. This involved throwing three rowan berries into the air, three at the

Wolf, and three into his own mouth. The magician Merlin, having been driven mad by the terrible sights he had seen during the battle between the armies of King Peredur and Gwenddoleu, retired to the woods to live as a hermit. His main companion was a very old Wolf who had lived in the woods for many years, and with this guide Merlin took on the role of the lord of the animals.

The Roman myth of Romulus and Remus, who were suckled and raised by a she-wolf, has a parallel in the Irish legend of King Cormac, who was also suckled by Wolves and accompanied by them throughout his life. The Celts seemed to view the Wolf in a very favourable light, and the beast was particularly associated with the god Cernunnos, Lord of the Animals, who had a Wolf as one of his closest companions. The Irish goddess Brigid, and her later form of St Brigit, is also often depicted in the company of a Wolf.

The Wolf has a very strong transformative association, which existed long before Hollywood. The Irish goddess Morrigan took the form of a Wolf in order to taunt her old adversary CuChulainn before battle. An old Irish story tells of triplet sisters who would take on the shape of Wolves and roam the countryside, killing and causing mayhem wherever they went. The harper Cascarach was asked to destroy the troublesome beasts. Cascarach knew that, as they were of a single birth, the girls could only be killed with a single blow, and only when they were in their human form. The harper used his musical skills to charm the three Wolves to him and, enchanted as they were by the music, he persuaded them that they would be better able to hear and appreciate the sound if they changed out of their Wolf skins. As they regained human form, Cascarach struck with a spear which passed through the heart of each of the three girls, and so they were destroyed. Even in the earliest stories, werewolves were notoriously difficult to kill.

The Norse people viewed the Wolf in a slightly different light, with admiration and fear for its ferocity. Many Saxon and Danish kings used the word for 'Wolf' as part of their name and title. The Wolf had a strong association with battle; an old saying held that whoever lost the battle, the Wolf always won, feeding on the carcasses and bodies of the dead. Odin had two companion

Wolves named Freki and Geri, and the terrible giantess Hyrrokin rode a monster Wolf using vipers as reins. In Teutonic myth, the Valkyries also used Wolves as mounts. The Wolf Hati (meaning 'hatred') constantly pursues the sun across the sky, while behind him the Wolf Skoll ('repulsion') chases the moon. It was believed that each Wolf would eventually catch its quarry and devour it. They occasionally each get close enough to take a bite, causing an eclipse.

The most terrible of all Wolves, the embodiment of evil, was Fenrir, the massive son of the god Loki and the giantess Angrboda. The gods determined that Fenrir should be bound until he should free himself at Ragnarok and kill Odin. The strongest iron chains were wound around the Wolf, but Fenrir snapped each one. Eventually, the gods called upon the dwarfs for help, and they made a magical chain, not from iron but from 'the sound a cat makes when it moves, a woman's beard, the roots of a mountain, the sinews of a bear, the breath of a fish, and a bird's spittle'. Fenrir was suspicious of the chain, and refused to be bound in it until Odin's son Tyr agreed to hold his hand in Fenrir's mouth as hostage against the Wolf's release. The chain proved effective, however, and Tyr lost his hand as the price for binding the terrible Wolf.

CHARACTERISTICS: *Community; Teaching; Co-operation; Society; Knowledge; Nurturing; Companionship; Instinct; Victory; Ferocity; Guidance; Intelligence*

In a spread, the Wolf can represent the importance of community and the ability to co-operate with others. It can also symbolize interaction with others in the form of guidance or teaching. The Wolf has a strong personality, often using its abilities for the good of society, but it also carries the potential for destructiveness if allowed to become too dominant.

SPIRAL PATH MEANING: *THE MENTOR*

The Wolf, as a teacher, holds compassion for humankind and teaches it its place within the community of animals, trees and plants. It teaches you, in turn, to take on the role of teacher, to share your insights and experiences with others.

Redbreast

◆

KINGDOM: Purity
TRINE: Compassion
TEACHING: Sharer of Hardship

MYTHOLOGY AND FOLKLORE

The Redbreast – or robin as it is now more familiarly known – has a long association with humankind. It was linked in early culture with the turning of the seasons and with fire. Perhaps the boldness of the Redbreast in its dealings with humans has bred this affection – the bird is well known for sitting patiently on a bough waiting for a gardener to turn over some tasty morsel for its lunch, and in some places it is called the 'ploughman's bird'. Or perhaps the bird's endurance had an influence, the fact that it chose to share the harsh winter with the people of Albion rather than migrate to warmer climes like some of its less hardy fellows.

Most folk legends agree that to harm a Redbreast is extremely bad luck, and may result in your house being struck by lightning, various ills of the hand or legs, or even death. In Norse mythology, the Redbreast was the bird of the god Thor, and was under his particular protection. A number of folk sayings warn against the danger of harming the birds; for example an old Scottish rhyme:

> The Robin and the Lintil, the Laverock and the Wren,
> Them that harries their nests will never thrive again.

(The lintil is the linnet and the laverock is the skylark. Notice the association between the robin and the wren – this is a very common pairing.)

The protectiveness towards and reverence for the bird seems to have arisen from its association with compassion and with helping people. There are several stories that tell how the robin got its red breast, but in all cases they involve compassion and self-sacrifice. In early British and Breton stories, the Redbreast was one of a relay of birds which brought a burning brand from the sun, giving the gift of fire to humankind. The Redbreast held the brand rather too close to the end, singeing its feathers. Until recently, a game known as 'robin's alight' was played in Scotland and Cornwall, in which a burning brand was passed from hand to hand; the person holding the brand when the flame went out had to pay a forfeit, which may well echo earlier rites to select human sacrifice.

French and Welsh stories tell that the red breast was obtained while the bird was trying to quench the fires of hell with its wings – the Welsh word for the robin, 'bronrhuddyn', means 'scorched breast'. A later association tells how the robin's breast was pierced while it was attempting to remove the Crown of Thorns from the head of Jesus. Another old story tells that if Redbreasts come upon an unattended human corpse in the countryside or woods, they will cover the body with leaves and moss. This legend has survived to the present day in the well-known pantomime 'Babes in the Wood', in which the two children, lost and alone in the woods, are given a protective covering of leaves by the birds to keep them warm while they are sleeping – a rather gentler form of the original, more morbid, belief.

Redbreasts are often depicted on Christmas cards. This reflects traditions linking the bird with the beginning of the new year. On New Year's Eve, the Redbreast would kill the wren – the representative of the old year – to let in the new season. The familiar nursery rhyme 'Who Killed Cock Robin' may contain elements of this early belief, although the modern form we know now was invented as an 18th century political satire. In medieval times, part of the 'wassail' ceremony to celebrate Christmas and welcome the new year involved hanging offerings of food for the Redbreasts, which were seen as good spirits and positive omens for the coming year.

CHARACTERISTICS: *Compassion; Boldness; Daring; Courage; Bluster; Stamina; Companionship; Friendship; Loyalty; Protection*

In a spread, the Redbreast represents the boldness and courage to show compassion for others, and the strength to help by actively sacrificing your own needs. It can also symbolize the fortitude to endure the troubles of the world, or an enduring friendship. The Redbreast's strength of spirit can enable it to give support to others until no longer needed.

SPIRAL PATH MEANING: *SHARER OF HARDSHIP*

The Redbreast teaches compassion for all living things, and offers the strength to understand and share their pain.

Otter

◆

KINGDOM: Purity
TRINE: Nurturing
TEACHING: The Child of Joy

MYTHOLOGY AND FOLKLORE

The Otter's unusual lifestyle and habits caused considerable confusion in early times over exactly what kind of animal it was. There were long-running discussions among the Celtic Christian clergy over whether the Otter should be classified as fish, which could be eaten during Lent, or meat, which could not. Another name for the Otter is the 'water dog', and to a certain extent the Otter shares some of the symbolism of the hound. The Irish hero CuChulainn, whose geas forbade the eating of dog flesh, was eventually killed after breaking the prohibition; as he lay dying by a stream, an Otter lapped at his blood.

The Otter often appears as a guide or helper, particularly to those heroes undertaking sea voyages and quests. The navigators Maelduine and Brendan were both assisted by friendly Otters who brought them food in extremity, as were a number of ancient hermits and holy men. St Cuthbert would habitually pray with his feet in the sea at Lindisfarne, after which two Otters would appear and dry his feet with their fur. Having performed this service, the Otters would wait patiently for the saint's blessing, which they would then carry back with them into the sea.

The Otter's skin was much prized for its waterproof qualities, and was the traditional covering for the Celtic harp. Irish Myth tells of the King of the Otters, who was invulnerable until killed by the hero Muiredach. Wearing a coat he had made from the pelt of the Otter, Muiredach was protected from all harm.

The Otter was also a popular transformative beast, and was one of the forms taken by Ceridwen in her shape-changing duel with the bard Taliesin. In Shetland and the north of Scotland the Otter, along with the horse, was one of the forms favoured by the kelpies, who would lure unsuspecting mortals into the sea and thence into the Underworld. In Norse myth, a shape-changing Otter caused problems for the three gods Odin, Loki and Honir. Coming across an Otter dozing by a pool with a freshly-killed salmon, Loki killed the beast with a stone, congratulating himself for obtaining the flesh of both beasts with a single throw. The Otter, however, turned out to be the animal form of the eldest son of the magician Hreidmar, who overcame the three gods and demanded compensation for his son's death. Loki was charged with obtaining sufficient red gold to fill and cover completely a bag made from the unfortunate Otter's pelt. This he did by stealing the gold from the dwarf Andvari, and the gods were released; but Loki had tricked Hreidmar at the last, as the gold itself carried a dire curse.

The Otter's grace in and out of the water, its sense of fun and play, and its inquisitiveness and almost human characteristics have endeared it to many. Nevertheless, the Otter does have its enemies among humankind, particularly those whose livelihood depends upon fishing, who regard the Otter as vermin; in the past, fishermen would hunt the beast using a three-pronged spear. It has also been hunted for its attractive and waterproof coat, and in some parts of Britain people still hunt the beast for 'sport' with packs of Otter hounds. Recent changes in habitat have led to the Otter becoming increasingly rare in the wild.

CHARACTERISTICS: *Emotions; Joy; Play; Fun; Delight; Innocence; Childlike Enjoyment; Pure Heart; Guidance; Nurturing; Parenthood; Simple Pleasures; Helpfulness*

In a spread, the Otter represents an openness and emotional expressiveness, and a childlike wonder and joy at the world and at life in general. It can represent the joy of parenthood, and nurturing the joy of life in others. The Otter has a huge capacity for fun and play, taking enjoyment from the most simple and mundane tasks.

SPIRAL PATH MEANING: *THE CHILD OF JOY*

The Otter teaches the nurturing of the child within, allowing childlike joy and wonder to return to adult life and responsibilities.

Cow

◆

KINGDOM: Purity
TRINE: Nurturing
TEACHING: The Nurturer

MYTHOLOGY AND FOLKLORE

Although a few herds of wild cattle can still be found in Britain, it was the domesticated Cow that played a vital part in the economy of early societies and which has one of the longest associations with humankind. It was the main source of nourishment and wealth, and indeed was used as a kind of currency, with the price of slaves and of brides being set in Cows.

The major Celtic festivals of Beltaine and Samhain were determined by the needs of the cattle herds – Beltaine marked the time during the spring when the Cows would be taken to summer pasture, and Samhain marked the winter slaughter. The major roads and tracks across the country, before the coming of the Romans, were determined by the cattle droves. In Ireland, and later in border regions of Britain, cattle raids were an essential way of life and determined the supremacy of clans and kings. The Irish epic *Tain Bo Cuailnge* (the Cattle Raid of Cooley) recounts the story of one such raid, and is one of the most important tales in early Irish literature. Small wonder, then, that tales of supernatural and faerie cattle show them to be the embodiment of plenty, a cornucopia of milk and meat forever replenished.

From earliest times, the Cow has been associated with the archetypal Earth Mother image, and the beast's horns have reinforced a link with lunar goddesses. In Ireland, the Cow was the special beast of the nurturing goddess Brigid (later St Brigit), and also of the goddess Boann, from whose name comes the present river name Boyne. Like the pig, the Cow was such a great gift that it was felt to have otherworldly origins, and there are many tales of faerie cattle stolen by mortals from their magical owners. These Cows were generally red or white in colour, and universally gave great quantities of milk.

The Irish god Dagda owned a magical Cow named Ocean, which had the ability to summon all the other cattle in Ireland to follow her, and which enabled the people of the Tuatha de Danaan to regain all the cattle stolen from them in a raid by the legendary Fomorians. The sea-god Manannan also had a number of Cows which came from the sea and gave three times the normal yield of milk, but if any mortal farmer offended them they would return to the sea taking their wealth with them. Manannan's foster-daughter Ethniu lived on the milk from these Cows, and in the battle of the White Strand the Irish warriors of the Fianna lived for a whole year on the fresh milk from a magical herd of cattle belonging to Credhe. St Brigit herself was said to have been fed as a baby on the milk of a Cow of Underworld origin.

Faerie cattle – called Crudh Mara in the Highlands of Scotland – would sometimes be left as gifts for mortals, and could be identified by their round ears. In Ireland, a sacred white heifer would appear on May Day to bring luck to the farmer. But these gifts were not to be abused. Stories are told in Ireland and England of a magical Cow who came from the sky and gave milk freely to whomever desired it. An evil witch, however, milked her into a sieve, which of course could never become full, at which the Cow left the human world for ever. Witches were blamed for milking dry ordinary Cows as well, and it was believed that this could be achieved at a distance by the witch casting a spell and making 'milking motions' in the air; alternatively, the witch might take the form of a hedgehog or a hare and suck the Cow dry directly.

The gift of a Cow was a particularly valuable and important gesture, providing wealth and sustenance to the recipient. Some people believed that if a man gave a Cow to the poor during the course of his lifetime, the spirit of the animal would appear to guide his soul to paradise on his death.

In Norse myth, the Cow was an even stronger symbol of the

nourisher and giver of life. The primeval Cow Audumla was said to have sprung from the ice at the beginning of time along with Ymir, the frost-giant. Ymir fed on the four rivers of milk that flowed from Audumla's teats, and the Cow ate the ice itself. As she licked away at the ice, Audumla formed from it the shape of the first man – Buri, grandfather of Odin.

In some parts of the country, red Cows were regarded as particularly protective and beneficial, and were also associated with the dawn. The milk of a red Cow was held to have healing properties, and even the cowpats could be used as poultices against sores and diseases of the skin. In Lancashire, the Milky Way was known as Cow's Lane.

Many people still believe that, at midnight on Christmas Eve, all Cows turn eastwards and kneel to welcome the birth of Jesus, just as they did in the stable at Bethlehem. Some hold that this actually happens on the eve of 6th January, the 'old' date for Christmas, and see such action by the Cows as proof that the older date is the correct one. According to one story, the Cow at Bethlehem covered the new-born Jesus with straw and warmed him with her breath during the cold night, which is why the Cow's breath always smells sweet.

CHARACTERISTICS: *Gentleness; Fertility; Domesticity; Parenthood; Love; Caring; Nurturing; Well-being; Talent; Self-worth; Wealth; Nourishment*

In a spread, the Cow represents the desire and ability to care for and nurture others, gaining pleasure from giving of yourself for others' benefit. It may also represent talents and gifts which, if used wisely, can lead to fulfilment and wealth. The Cow takes life at its own pace, able to share its abundance with others.

SPIRAL PATH MEANING: *THE NURTURER*

The Cow teaches a willingness to share your talents and gifts with others, and the capacity to take on the role of nurturer in the confidence and certainty of your ability to provide.

Pig

KINGDOM: Purity

TRINE: Nurturing

TEACHING: The Initiator

MYTHOLOGY AND FOLKLORE

For many centuries the Pig represented one of the most powerful and important symbols to inhabitants of Britain. The Pig provided sustenance, both physical and spiritual, and epitomized the desirable attributes of ferocity, bravery, vitality and fertility. Enjoying similar status to the revered Boar (see page 26), little wonder that Pigs were thought to originate from a supernatural origin, and that their flesh formed the basis of feasts in the Underworld. The swineherds who looked after their needs were held in great esteem by Celtic society.

According to the *Mabinogion*, the first Pigs to be seen in Britain were a gift to Pryderi, Lord of Dyfed, from the King of the Underworld. Math, the Lord of Gwynedd, determined to acquire these strange new beasts, whose flesh was reputed to be sweeter than that of any other animal, and sent his nephews Gwydion and Gilfaethwy to Pryderi's court to obtain some of the Pigs. The quest was fulfilled through a magical deception, but on learning of the deceit, Pryderi pursued the brothers, resulting in a terrible war between Dyfed and Gwynedd. Gwydion and Pryderi met in single combat, and Pryderi was killed; but Gwydion and Gilfaethwy were dishonoured by the rape of Math's handmaiden, Goewin. As punishment for their crime, Math transformed Gwydion and Gilfaethwy into the male and female of three separate animals for a year each, and in each shape they bore a child; firstly, as a stag and a hind, then as a boar and a sow, and finally as a wolf and a wolf-bitch. The son they bore in pig-shape was transformed back into human form and named Hychdwn the 'noble Boar'.

The Irish sea-god Manannan was known to keep a magical herd of Pigs in his Underworld kingdom. Every animal killed and eaten in the feast each evening would be magically reborn the next morning. Any human eating the flesh of these animals would achieve immortality. The flesh was not easy to cook, however, as the water in which the Pigs were placed would not boil until a truth were spoken for each quarter of the Pig.

The Celtic sow-goddess Ceridwen, 'the old white one', represented inspiration and fertility. Like the sow who eats her own young, Ceridwen was also represented as the hag and devourer, who held the cauldron of rebirth and initiation. Ceridwen was the mother of Afagddu, the ugliest boy in the world, and she resolved to compensate for this by brewing for him a magical potion in her cauldron of wisdom and inspiration. The potion took a year to prepare, and during this time it was tended and stirred by the youth Gwion. One day, however, as Gwion was stirring the brew, three drops splashed onto his fingers, and Gwion instinctively sucked the burn, immediately gaining great knowledge and power. Enraged, Ceridwen pursued the youth, and each used their power to transform themselves into a series of fleeing and pursuing animal shapes; firstly a greyhound and a hare, then an otter and a fish, then a hawk and a bird. Finally, Gwion changed into a grain of corn and Ceridwen, as a hen, ate him. Nine months later, the spirit of Gwion was reborn to Ceridwen as the bard Taliesin. This shape-changing battle is one of a number recounted in Celtic legend, and represents the stages of initiation.

In many stories, the Pig represents a guide to knowledge that must be revealed. When the Welsh hero Llew, betrayed by his flower-maiden bride Blodeuwedd, was sitting badly wounded in a tree in the shape of an eagle, it was a foraging Pig feeding on the rotting pieces of flesh falling from the tree that guided the magician Gwydion to the spot. King Bladud, when deposed from his sovereignty because of his leprosy, became a swineherd to a collection of scabby and diseased Pigs. When Bladud let them bathe in the mud at a spring in the place now called Bath, he noticed that their sores were immediately healed, and took advantage of the healing properties himself to cure his disease and regain the throne.

Pigs have widely been thought of as reliable predictors of the weather, and were believed to be able to 'see the wind' and warn of imminent storms. They were also common witch-animals, and there are several documented accounts of Pigs being tried and executed in the belief that they were actually witches in animal form. A garland of rowan would be placed around the animal's neck or in its sty to protect the Pig from the effects of witchcraft.

In Ireland Pigs were considered particularly lucky, a belief that still survives today, as they held for the poor people the same values of sustenance and prosperity as they did for the early Celts. Carvings and mascots of the beast were widely used as luck talismans, yet these symbols were considered effective only if some part were broken, and, as a result, are often found missing an ear or a leg.

CHARACTERISTICS: *Vitality; Sustenance; Fertility; Honour; Status; Truth; Initiation; Necessary Knowledge; Wealth; Abundance; Self-indulgence; Intelligence; Wilfulness*

In a spread, the Pig represents the ability to sustain and support others. It can also mean the need for recognition and status, and the strength to renew energy reserves. The Pig may appear placid and self-indulgent, but it has the potential for wilfulness and aggression.

SPIRAL PATH MEANING: *THE INITIATOR*

The Pig offers initiation, nurturing the soul and making it grow. The Pig shatters perceptions, but, like a mother with a child, makes you face new and often frightening experiences in order to grow into full awareness.

Hare

◆

KINGDOM: Purity

TRINE: Inspiration

TEACHING: Bringer of Inspired
Madness

MYTHOLOGY AND FOLKLORE

The Hare – and to a lesser extent its later associate, the rabbit, which was introduced into Britain by the Normans – was long regarded as a symbol of fecundity and sexual pleasure. It was closely associated with the moon and its goddesses, particularly Oestra, the Teutonic goddess of the moon who gave her name to the Easter festival, and is often depicted as hare-headed. Oestra's Hare laid the egg of new life to herald the rebirth of the year – a rare example of an ancient belief carrying through to modern times in stories of the Easter Bunny who distributes eggs in the springtime.

The patterns in the full moon are said to represent the shape of a Hare, and because of its lunar associations, the Hare was also regarded as a messenger of the gods, and as such was sacred to the Roman Mercury. Its sexual attributes also led to its use in rituals associated with Venus and Eros. The Celts held it sacred to gods of the moon and the hunt and, according to Julius Caesar, kept it in such esteem that they would not eat it – a tradition not retained by the invading Romans, who considered it a delicacy. Norse myth represented the moon goddess as being attended by a procession of Hares bearing lanterns, and Freyja – another fertility goddess – also had Hares as attendants. The Hare was believed to change its sex at the start of each new year, alternating between male and female throughout its life.

The Hare was widely used as a divinatory animal, perhaps

partly because of the belief that young Hares are born with their eyes open and never close them again, even to blink or sleep. The Celtic war-leader Boudicca kept a Hare for divination, releasing it from beneath her cloak prior to each battle and watching its path to predict the outcome.

Probably because of its 'undesirable' early associations, the medieval Christian view changed the Hare into a beast of ill-omen. Witches in the shape of Hares would suck a cow dry of milk, and there were many reports of wounds inflicted on a Hare caught in such an act being found the following day on the local wise-woman or crone. A witch in Hare's form could only be killed with a silver crucifix or, later, a silver bullet. Among sailors, the Hare was considered so unlucky that even to mention its name at sea would bring disaster, so other names were invented to refer safely to the animal. A Hare crossing the path was considered extremely unlucky in some places, especially for a pregnant woman who would then miscarry or produce a child with a 'harelip'. To ward off all this bad luck, it was wise to carry as a charm a Hare's foot (or later a rabbit's foot), preferably from the left rear leg, but the consequences of losing such a charm were dire indeed. Children in some places still say 'white rabbit' three times on the first day of the month for luck. In Cornwall, white Hares were believed to contain the spirits of young girls who had died of grief as a result of romantic disappointments.

The Hare is also associated with 'madness' or with manic behaviour. A well-known example is Lewis Carroll's March Hare in *Alice in Wonderland* who incidentally, was also a messenger in *Through the Looking Glass*, in this case for the White Queen. This reputation is mostly a result of its well-observed wild habits during the spring mating season, when pairs of the animals may be seen 'boxing' or leaping into the air – normally a reaction by a female Hare to a male's persistent sexual behaviour. Adult Hares show little concern or care for their young and do not form family groups, only loose collections with a dominant male hierarchy fighting over the available females.

Ancient beliefs concerning the Hare have survived into modern traditions and stories with their original meanings providing an almost unbroken link with the earliest associations.

CHARACTERISTICS: *Physical Activity; Obsession; Sexuality; Fertile Ideas; Enthusiasm; Inspired Madness; Rebelliousness; Unconventionality; Energy; Carefree Attitudes*

In a spread, the Hare represents enthusiasm for life, the awakening of new energy and inspiration, and the expressions of this energy in unconventional ways. It may also represent obsession; the compulsion of the Hare's madness needs to be tempered with responsibility. The Hare tends to follow a whim without thinking through the consequences, and prefers to live a carefree existence.

SPIRAL PATH MEANING: *BRINGER OF INSPIRED MADNESS*

The Hare brings wild inspiration, which rushes through the body like rising sap, demanding expression in any way possible.

Swan

◆

KINGDOM: Purity

TRINE: Inspiration

TEACHING: Song of·Inspired Love

MYTHOLOGY AND FOLKLORE

The Swan frequently appeared in ·early stories as a powerful transformative beast. Young maidens were particularly able to take the form of Swans, or be transformed by magic into Swans. These metamorphosed humans could usually be recognized by the gold and silver collars worn around their necks, and this image persisted throughout Greek, Roman, Celtic and Teutonic myth. The Swan also symbolized glorious and faithful love, and was often the form chosen by lovers in expeditions or escapes.

In Roman legend, the Swan was sacred to Apollo, and indeed his very soul was said to have become a Swan. It was also associated with Aphrodite/Venus, whose chariot was drawn by a flight of Swans, reinforcing the beast's sexual association. Significantly, Zeus's rape of Leda was accomplished in the form of a Swan. Following the rape, Leda produced two eggs, from one of which sprang the divine twins Castor and Pollux, and from the other Clytemnestra and Helena. The Swan's links with Zeus and other thunder-gods may also account for the later superstition that Swans' eggs will only hatch in a thunder storm, requiring the strike of the lightning to crack the shell.

The legend of the 'swan song' also originates from the Greek and Roman period. Socrates and Plato, among others, referred to the belief that a Swan would make no sound throughout its life, except in the moments before its death when it would sing a song of great beauty. Its song was therefore associated both with prophecy, in knowing the time of its own death, and, through its association with Apollo, with music. The great musician Orpheus was also said to have chosen the form of a Swan after his death.

In Celtic myth, Swans are associated with the goddess Brigid, and feature in a number of tales of transformation. The link with music also appears to have been maintained throughout this period, as Swan skin and feathers were traditionally used to make the ritual cloak of the poet. In some stories, the song of the Swan held magical properties which would cause sleep in mortals, and many tales of love and jealousy feature Swan transformations.

In the Irish story *The Dream of Oenghus*, the god Oenghus falls madly in love with the maiden Caer Ibormeith who, with 150 of her companions, alternates each year between human and Swan shape. With the maiden's father opposed to the match, Oenghus learns that the only way he can possess her is to take her in Swan form, and so transforms himself into a Swan on the day before the girl is due to assume her human shape for another year. The two lovers fly together three times around the lake. They sing a magical song which causes Caer Ibormeith's father and his household to sleep for three days and nights, allowing them to escape.

A Celtic story with a less happy ending is that of the children of Lir, who were transformed into Swans by their jealous stepmother. The children were condemned to spend 900 years in Swan form – 300 years in each of three locations around Ireland and Scotland – and could only resume human form when a prince from the north married a princess from the south, and a church bell was rung in Ireland. Eventually these things came to pass, and it was the sound of St Patrick's bell, heralding the introduction of Christianity in Ireland, which eventually freed the children from the spell. As soon as their human form was restored, however, the enchantment of their 900-year life was broken, and they immediately died of old age.

Teutonic myth placed great importance on the Swan-maidens, the Valkyries, who could fly through the air in Swan-form, and, whenever they chose, could discard their plumage to regain human shape. Any man who could steal this plumage while the

Swans were in human form could, however, command the Valkyries and impose his will upon them. This theme forms the basis of the story on which Richard Wagner based his well-known opera, *The Ring of the Nibelung*, in which the Valkyrie Brynhild, with eight of her companions, carelessly allows the mortal King Agnar to seize their plumage. Agnar forces the nine Valkyries to assist in his war against his enemy Hjalmgunnar. As a punishment, Odin has Brynhild pricked with a magic thorn which causes her to fall into a deep slumber – reminiscent of that caused by the song of the Swan in Irish stories – and imprisons her in a dwelling encircled by a wall of flame. She is eventually rescued by the hero Sigurd, love once again defying all odds.

The themes of faithfulness and magical song also appear in the Norse myth of the Swan-maiden Kara, who would hover in battle above her human lover Helgi and enchant his enemies with her song, allowing him to triumph. On one occasion, however, Kara flew a little too close to Helgi and was fatally wounded by his upraised sword. In other Norse stories, Swans were associated with the sky-god Freyr; their white plumage as they flew around his chariot could be seen in the white cirrus clouds.

CHARACTERISTICS: *Faithfulness; Partnership; Loving Sexual Relationship; True Love; Purity; Music; Inspiration; Transformation; Serenity; Selflessness; Grace; Calm*

In a spread, the Swan represents the strength of love to overcome adversity, and the gaining of inspiration through true love. It can represent a test of love; a willingness to give up everything for love, or to be faithful against the odds. The Swan gives itself totally to any relationship, and demands the same commitment in return.

SPIRAL PATH MEANING: *SONG OF INSPIRED LOVE*

The Swan teaches the abandonment of self through true love, and the inspiration that results from this abandonment.

Eagle

◆

KINGDOM: Purity

TRINE: Inspiration

TEACHING: Guide to Spiritual
Inspiration

MYTHOLOGY AND FOLKLORE

The Eagle is a powerful and almost universally recognized solar symbol, the 'sun-bird' which represents ascension, inspiration and freedom, temporal and spiritual power. It is often depicted in combat with or clutching more earthly animals, such as the lion, bull or hare, and particularly the serpent, representing the triumph of the mind and spirit over the mundane physical world. An early tradition held that Eagles were able to stare continuously at the sun without blinking. Fledgling Eagles would be taken close to the sun and forced to stare at it as a ritual initiation; any who blinked would be considered weak and unworthy, and allowed to fall to their deaths.

The Greeks and Romans held that the Eagle was the only bird to be found in the heavens with the gods. Originally the Eagle was the special bird of the god Pan, but it was later associated with the powerful sky-god Jupiter. The Eagle is recognized as a bringer of storms and thunder, and in Welsh legend Eagles were said to sit on the slopes of Mount Snowdon and flap their wings to create winds and storms. The bird was also used as a messenger by Apollo, and as an emblem of the solar-god Mithras.

The Roman emperors adopted the all-conquering Eagle as a symbol of imperial power, and the Eagle standard was an important icon to the Roman armies who invaded Britain. Indeed the standard formed the basis of a shrine for the Roman soldiery, and was a focus for their religious worship. When a Roman emperor died, an Eagle was released as part of the funeral ceremonies, its flight to freedom representing the escape of the emperor's spirit from the physical plane.

The Celts saw in the Eagle a representation of old knowledge. In the story of the search for the Mabon, the Eagle was the second-oldest animal on Earth, who pointed the way to the salmon who knew the location of the Mabon's prison. The association between the Eagle and the salmon occurs in several stories. The poets Fintan and Tuan Mac Carill both spent some time in Eagle-shape before settling on their final animal forms as salmon. Both animals were considered repositories of ancient knowledge and lore stretching back almost to the beginning of time. King Arthur was reported to have engaged in a long dialogue with an Eagle who was actually his transformed nephew Ewilod, and who displayed an amazing wisdom and knowledge of the Otherworld. Arthur's hidden sleeping place, where he rests against the day when he will again be needed, is said to be guarded by an Eagle. Adam and Eve are also reputed to live on in the form of Eagles.

The Eagle's long life was reputedly maintained by renewal and rejuvenation rather than simple longevity. An old legend tells that, when an Eagle was growing old, it would fly right up to the sun so that its feathers were scorched, before plunging into the sea and re-emerging as a young bird. Irish legend tells how the hero Maelduine observed an Eagle renewing itself in this way in a secret lake. The Eagle was also reputed to be immune from death in all the usual ways, and could die only from starvation when, at a great age, its beak would grow inwards, preventing it from feeding.

In Norse myth, an Eagle sits at the top of Yggdrasil, the tree of life, representing the summit of spiritual achievement. The Eagle is constantly at war with the serpent which lies at Yggdrasil's roots. Together with the wolf and the raven, the Eagle was one of the Norse beasts of battle, and appeared on many standards and in honorific names. A particularly nasty form of Norse ritual execution was the 'blood Eagle', whereby a victim's rib cage would be split open and his lungs – symbolic of Eagle's wings – removed from the body cavity. The Eagle was sacred to Odin, who occasionally took its form, as did the North Wind.

Despite its power and wisdom, the Eagle was also noted for its pride, which could lead at times to its defeat by lesser animals. Although the Eagle is generally regarded as the king of the air, one legend tells how this title was claimed by the wren, who won it in a contest to see which bird could fly the highest (see page 41). In the Celtic story of the Hawk of Achill, the Eagle is tricked from its warm nest by the hawk and sent on a fruitless quest to find out which animal could remember the coldest night. On its return, the Eagle finds that the hawk has killed all its chicks and usurped the nest.

At one time Eagles were thought not to lay eggs but to give birth to live chicks with great difficulty. To ease the pain of their labour, Eagles made use of a magical stone, which they would carry back to their nests. These 'Eagle stones', supposedly collected from the Eagles' nests, were highly prized as talismans by women who wore them for protection during their own pregnancy and labour.

CHARACTERISTICS: *Inspiration; Intellect; Ambition; Power; Perception; Awareness; Attainment; Victory; Spirit; Knowledge; Freedom; Wisdom; Renewal; Rejuvenation; Pride; Vocation; Spirituality; Initiation*

In a spread, the Eagle represents the triumph of mind and spirit over physical restrictions, and the strength of mind to gain and use power. It may also represent the need to renew your life by attaining spiritual insight and freedom from the restraints of the everyday world. The Eagle has the ability to perceive and understand the true nature of things, but it may also have a tendency towards excessive pride in its abilities.

SPIRAL PATH MEANING: *GUIDE TO SPIRITUAL INSPIRATION*

The Eagle guides you to the highest level of your own awareness, linking you with the divine within yourself and all things.

Toad

◆

KINGDOM: Purity

TRINE: Transformation

TEACHING: Jewel of the Self

MYTHOLOGY AND FOLKLORE

The Toad, and its cousin the frog, are perhaps best known to us nowadays in two roles: firstly as the familiars of witches, and as an important ingredient in their evil spells; and secondly as a transformative beast, whose ugly and repulsive exterior may reveal a beautiful and highly desirable prince when released by a maiden's kiss. The latter image, which has a mainly European origin, is also probably a metaphor for adolescent sexual awakening. Medieval alchemists held that the Toad represented the primal elements of nature.

The earliest stories seem to represent the Toad as an evil and ill-omened beast. The Toad's preferred habitat of watery and muddy places have associated it with the Underworld and lunar powers. The Celts, however, seem to have held the frog in sufficient regard to name it the Lord of the Earth. They also associated it with healing waters, and used both frogs and toads in cures for ills as diverse as warts and epilepsy.

The Toad quickly gained a reputation as a venomous beast. The common English species have glands that secrete a foul-tasting liquid to deter predators, but this is in fact a purely protective device and not poisonous. The Toad was also said to carry in its head a precious stone, the Borax Stone, which was widely sought as an antidote to all poisons. In *As You Like It*, Shakespeare writes:

> Sweet are the uses of adversity,
> Which, like the toad, ugly and venomous,
> Wears yet a precious jewel in his head.

The Toad also has a strong history of use in divination. The Romans were said to use the animal as a sort of direction-finder or compass; placing a naked dagger-blade on the animal's back was said to make it hop around until the dagger pointed due north! In Cornish tin mines, the appearance of a Toad indicated that the miners would find a good seam. Frogs and Toads are also traditional rain-bringers, and rites including whipping or killing the animals were supposed to cause precipitation.

The frog also features prominently in fertility and love magic, with its entrails and bones used as love potions or divinatory aids for young girls. Perhaps it is this aspect that influenced the familiar frog-prince fairy tales of the brothers Grimm and others. In many medieval paintings Toads were used as representatives of evil licentiousness. They were often depicted covering both male and female genitals – yet another example of the medieval church twisting earlier, positive, pagan aspects of fertility and sexuality and presenting them as evil.

This negative image of the frog in England seems to have intensified in the late 16th century, when Queen Elizabeth I was being courted by a Frenchman, the Duke of Alençon, whom she affectionately referred to as her 'frog'. (The English habit of using the term 'frog' for all Frenchmen did not come into common use until much later.) Many of Elizabeth's advisors disapproved of the match, and the 'frog' became a common satirical tool which persisted for many years after the Queen's death. Spenser and Shakespeare use the Toad as a symbol of sexual jealousy, and Milton uses it as a symbol for the Devil whispering temptations into Eve's ear.

The association of the Toad with the witch is perhaps the strongest image of all. Shakespeare's witches in *Macbeth* use a Toad as a vital ingredient in their brew, and frogs and Toads were, with cats, the most common form for a witch's familiar, and a favoured animal form for the witch herself.

Properly harnessed by a practitioner, the Toad's power could be used for protection. A dried frog could be worn in a bag around the neck to ward off harm, and a thief carrying a dead Toad would avoid capture. In the east of England, there was a belief that certain men could become 'Toadmen', possessing great power to control horses and other animals, which made them much in demand on farms. Becoming a Toadman meant undergoing a long, complex ritual involving the use of Toads' bones, but the charm was also believed to give these men great persuasive power over human beings, particularly women! Belief in Toadmen continued well into this century.

CHARACTERISTICS: *Hidden Beauty; Healing; Strong Sexuality; Protection; Fertility; Repression of Abilities; Tradition; Primal Instincts; Transformation*

In a spread, the Toad represents the ability to find beauty within oneself and self-acceptance, leading to physical and mental healing. It can also represent the need for help from others to find your true abilities and potential, and to bring out your best qualities. The Toad has the ability to look beyond the surface level, and the face it presents to the world may well be superficial, concealing hidden depths.

SPIRAL PATH MEANING: *JEWEL OF THE SELF*

The Toad teaches you to look beyond your own body and personality to find the inner beauty that lies within. It shows you how to allow the awareness of this beauty to transform you.

Dove

◆

KINGDOM: Purity

TRINE: Transformation

TEACHING: Expression of Love

MYTHOLOGY AND FOLKLORE

The Dove is a familiar modern symbol of peace and harmony. This association may be traced right back to Greek mythology, in which the Dove with an olive branch in its beak was an emblem of Aphrodite, goddess of love and beauty and mediator between heaven and earth. Together with swans, doves also drew the chariot of Venus, Aphrodite's Roman equivalent.

Perhaps because of their pure-white colour, Doves were universally regarded as a positive symbol, representing purity, harmony and faithfulness. Doves were reputed to pair for life, and the association with lovers has also been long-standing, with pairs of Doves a traditional wedding gift in some parts of eastern England until very recent times. The Christmas gift of 'two turtle Doves' in the well-known seasonal song is meant to bring luck and joy (the Dove was known as the 'turtle' until the 17th century).

A feminine symbol, the Dove was sacred to feminine forces including the Great Mother, Venus and the Virgin Mary. It also had strong oracular associations, and was regarded by the Romans as a messenger of the gods, as well as a useful carrier of more mundane communications in the same way as carrier pigeons. In Arthurian legend, the Dove was the emblem of the Grail messenger Kundrie, who was hideously ugly but extremely wise. Her garments were embroidered with Dove symbols. The Celts seem to have associated the bird with cults of healing. Images of Doves have been found at a number of healing temples and springs, particularly those that have a link with the Romano-Celtic Apollo – also an oracular figure.

Doves have traditionally been offered as sacrifice to a number of different gods, either in the traditional sense or by the release of the birds, whose flight pattern could then be used for divination. The Hebrews regarded the Dove as the only bird whose sacrifice was acceptable under the Laws of Moses, so Doves became the 'poor man's sacrifice', being relatively cheap and easy to obtain.

The Dove is the most frequently mentioned bird in the Old Testament, where it symbolizes simplicity and innocence. In the story of Noah and the Flood, the Dove brings back the leaf which confirms that land has reappeared. This is another instance of the Dove acting as a messenger and a voice for heavenly power.

In medieval times, seeing a Dove was considered a good omen, or a friendly warning. Miners would refuse to descend if a Dove was seen near a pit head. Doves should never be sold, but rather offered in love as a gift. It was believed that sick people would not die if they were lain on a mattress stuffed with Doves' feathers. And the Dove was the one transformative shape that could not be taken by the Devil or by witches – perhaps the reason why it retains such a positive image.

In modern times, the Dove has continued to symbolize peace and harmony, and has been adopted as the emblem or badge for a wide range of charities and international agencies working for peace. The release of Doves at major international sporting and cultural events is still used as a universally recognized symbol of friendship and co-operation.

CHARACTERISTICS: *Peace; Harmony; Healing; True Love; Simplicity; Innocence; Faithfulness; Truth; Naiveté; First Love; Freedom; Prophecy; Messenger*

In a spread, the Dove represents the ability to give love for the purest reasons. It can signify the peace, harmony healing and transformation that come through sharing love with people and with the land. There is, however, a danger of innocence leading to naiveté, which may be exploited by others. The Dove is a lover of peace and tranquility, who brings the message of harmony into the lives of others.

SPIRAL PATH MEANING: *EXPRESSION OF LOVE*

As the expression of love, the Dove teaches transformation through love: the personal transformation gained through a truly loving relationship, or the spiritual transformation experienced through divine love.

Butterfly

—— ◆ ——

MYTHOLOGY AND FOLKLORE

The Butterfly has long been regarded as a representation of the human soul, and is therefore generally treated with care and respect. The transformation from caterpillar to chrysalis and then to the beautiful, winged Butterfly has been widely seen as an allegory for death of the body and rebirth of the soul in paradise. In Gaelic areas, tradition held that the soul of the newly dead could sometimes be seen hovering over the corpse in the form of a Butterfly; this was an extremely positive omen for the well-being of the soul. If a golden Butterfly was observed at a funeral, the omen was particularly good, and could symbolize longevity for all the mourners present.

Celtic society also seems to have used the Butterfly as a symbol of renewal and rebirth. A particularly important festival in the Celtic year involved extinguishing the hearth fires of all the households in the community, then relighting them using a ceremonial brand from a communal bonfire. The Gaelic name given to this brand is the same as that for the Butterfly.

In Irish legend, the god Midhir loved and married the beautiful maiden Etain. Midhir, however, already had a wife, Fuamnach, who transformed her rival into a Butterfly, to be buffeted around the world by the wind for many years before eventually being reborn with no memory of her previous life. Midhir managed to track down Etain, now married in her new life to Eochaidh, High King of Ireland, and after reminding her with a kiss of their previous life together, the two lovers escaped from Eochaidh in the form of swans.

Some traditions tell that Butterflies are actually the souls of the dead waiting to enter purgatory, or in some cases the souls of unbaptized children, and for this reason they should never be harmed. In many parts of Britain, however, it was believed that the first Butterfly seen each year should be killed to ensure luck throughout the year. The colour of the first Butterfly to be seen was an important omen; if white, the observer would eat nothing but white bread (i.e. have the best of everything) all year, but if brown the year would be poor. A yellow Butterfly signified sickness in the year to come. In Westmorland, gangs of boys would hunt and kill white Butterflies – known as 'papishes' – on Oak Apple Day (29th May). Coloured Butterflies were known as 'King George's Butterflies', and were protected for that day.

Butterflies could also be negative omens. Seeing three flying together was widely regarded as a symbol of impending death, and on the Scottish borders, red Butterflies were thought to be witch-forms. Generally, however, the overriding symbols of transformation, renewal and rebirth symbolized by the Butterfly's particular life-cycle, as well as its natural beauty and fragility, ensured respect, reverence and protection for the creature. In recent times, it has become a symbol of softness, fragility and 'traditional' femininity, and is widely used on logos and branding for products wishing to emphasize these attributes.

CHARACTERISTICS: *Freedom; Beauty; Pleasure; Hope; The Soul; Regeneration; Transformation; Development*

In a spread, the Butterfly represents the freedom to move on the winds of change, although there is a warning that this may become a transient existence, 'flitting' around with no true direction or purpose. It may also symbolize development and transformation of the personality through experience. The Butterfly takes pleasure in beauty, but is not tied by the desire for the acquisition of lasting wealth.

SPIRAL PATH MEANING: *TRANSFORMATION OF SPIRIT*

The Butterfly teaches the transformation of spirit, freeing you from the confines of the body and the mundane. It brings beauty, love and light into the world.

Unicorn

◆

Spirit of the Kingdom of Purity

TEACHING: The Crown of Purity

MYTHOLOGY AND FOLKLORE

Belief in the existence of the fabulous Unicorn remained strong right up until the 18th and 19th centuries. Many people regarded its existence as a fact even though they had never seen one, in much the same way as they thought of the lion. The Unicorn was a creature of the moon – wise, graceful and beautiful. It represented purity, chastity and gentleness, and was a common subject for medieval tapestries and decorative art.

The first mention of the Unicorn as we would recognize it is by the Greek Ctesias. He described a creature like a horse with white body, dark-red head, and a single horn in the middle of the forehead with a white base, black centre and crimson tip – colours frequently associated with female lunar figures. Julius Caesar, in his 'Gallic Wars' commentary, mentions seeing a bull-sized animal shaped like a stag with a single tall, straight horn. The symbol of the Unicorn must have been familiar to Caesar, as it featured in Roman mythology associated with the lunar huntress Diana, who rode in a chariot drawn by eight Unicorns.

The Unicorn is variously described as resembling a goat, a stag, a horse or a bull. In most cases the colour of the body is white, but the colour of the horn may vary and the horn itself may be straight or spiralled. Some sources claimed that the Unicorn had cloven hooves, while others describe hooves like a horse. In medieval images of the Unicorn it often has a goat-like beard. In heraldry, it is depicted with the head and body of a horse, the legs of a stag and the tail of a lion, with a single straight or twisted horn on the forehead.

The value of the Unicorn lay principally in the magical properties of its horn, the 'alicorn', which had the power to detect and render harmless any poison, and to purify water. Cups and knife-handles made of the material were therefore much in demand by kings and rulers worried about the security of their position. The powdered horn was worth 10 times the equivalent weight of gold. Not surprisingly there was much trade in medieval times of artefacts reputedly made from Unicorn horn, although in many cases the material came from either the rhinoceros or, more commonly in Britain, the marine narwhal, which became known as the sea-unicorn. The standard test for a genuine horn was to use it to inscribe a circle on the ground, and place inside the circle a lizard or snake. If the beast remained trapped within the circle, the horn was truly that of the Unicorn.

Noble, solitary and intelligent, Unicorns lived alone in the deep forests and woodlands, acting as guardians and protectors for other woodland beasts. They could not be captured or killed by ordinary hunting methods, and could become savage and fierce when threatened, using the single horn to deadly effect on huntsmen and hounds. But the Unicorn had a fatal weakness which could be exploited by the cunning huntsman – it would become meek and gentle in the presence of a maiden, and would lay its head in the girl's lap, allowing itself to be captured or killed. Huntsmen would therefore lay traps for the beasts, using maidens as bait, sometimes sitting willingly and richly adorned to aid the hunt, at other times against their will, naked and tied to a tree. The obvious symbolism of the phallic horn in the lap of a young girl can also be seen as an allegory for puberty and sexual experience signalling the end of innocence and purity. Once captured, the Unicorn could be led meekly by using a halter made from the virgin's hair, and could be subdued permanently by shoeing it with silver.

The theme of the mighty Unicorn being overcome by innocence and chastity was popular in the medieval church. The image was used to represent the triumph of innocence, with the Unicorn sometimes representing the Devil, and sometimes a lover being lured to destruction. The innocence and purity of the beast also led it to be associated with the Virgin Mary and with Christ himself.

Many stories deal with the legendary battles between the lion and the Unicorn, with the Unicorn representing the moon, night, spring and feminine forces, and the lion symbolizing the sun, day, summer and masculinity. In all of these tales, the mystical Unicorn must eventually give way to the temporal power of the lion, as night gives way to day. King James IV of Scotland was so fascinated by the stories of the Unicorn that he adopted it as a device for his Royal coat of arms, and the battles of the lion and the Unicorn can be seen in some cases as a metaphor for the struggles between Scotland and the English, whose Royal device was a red lion.

The most abiding image of the Unicorn, however, is of a solitary nobleness and gentleness which responds to the purity in humans, sometimes to its own disadvantage. One belief was that every time a Unicorn died, a little more magic left the world.

CHARACTERISTICS: *Purity; Innocence; Virginity; Strength of Mind; Potential; Gentleness; Calm; Pride; Individual Power; Fierceness when Threatened; Solitude; Sovereignty; Unselfishness*

In a spread, the Unicorn represents power, inner beauty and gentleness – but only when the wild side of the personality is held in check. Otherwise it can mean pride, aggressiveness and stubbornness. The Unicorn has the ability to rise above the needs of the self.

SPIRAL PATH MEANING: *THE CROWN OF PURITY*

As the Spirit of the Kingdom of Purity, the Unicorn teaches purity and gentleness, and a guardianship for all creatures; it replaces the lost enchantment in the world through our hearts. Its horn removes the poisons of modern life that affect mind, body and spirit, bringing purity and rebirth.

PART 2

Totem and Companion Animals

Beasts of Albion is based on the ancient and traditional belief that animals are the companions and teachers of humankind. Using the card spreads and visualizations described in this section, you can find the Totem Animals that most closely represents your own inner self, and identify those Companion Animals whose attributes you need to develop within yourself. The previous section considered the imagery, mythology and tales associated with each particular beast; but each animal will bring its own story to you, telling of its own strengths, inner potentials and energies, and you will need to develop your own interpretation and understanding of the gifts it offers. By encountering the animal and becoming part of its story, the story will become part of you.

Meeting Your Totem Animal

The story offered by your Totem Animal is the story of your true Self. Your Totem can guide you to find your inner strengths and abilities, and to develop these qualities to help you in your everyday life. Like a Zodiac sign or birth chart, your Totem Animal is one you are born with, and generally remains with you throughout life, although it can occasionally change in certain circumstances. Some readers will already know their own Totem Animal, through a strong lifelong affinity for a particular creature or through having been guided to it in visualization or dreams. If you already know your Totem, and it is not one of the beasts represented in the deck, you should make use of the blank card supplied, as described in the Introduction, and include this in the deck for all future work.

If you do not know your own Totem, you may encounter it in a very simple way by using the cards. Sit in a comfortable, relaxed position in a quiet room where you will not be disturbed. Concentrate on yourself and on your perception of your Self. Become aware of your body, and draw your attention away from the everyday world. Shuffle the cards thoroughly. Keep shuffling and concentrating until you receive an impulse to stop. Turn over the top card from the deck. The animal depicted on this card is your Totem.

The animal representing your Totem may surprise you; make a note of your feelings towards the animal and how you think the animal applies to you. Some aspects of the animal's attributes and characteristics may not seem relevant; but these may be abilities or tendencies that have been hidden or repressed. Do not be dismayed if the animal has a somewhat negative image; in some cases, this will be the result of distorted modern media representation. Every animal has strengths you can call on, and lessons to be learned from sharing its story.

Meeting your Companion Animals

In addition to the Totem Animal, however, there are a number of Companion Animals. These beasts can be called upon to guide you to your strengths and abilities. Companion Animals change throughout your life, depending on your particular circumstances at the time. With their stories, they offer you energy to overcome obstacles and challenges, inspiration to solve problems or to create new ideas, and knowledge, compassion and understanding to help in relationships with others. The story of the Bear, for example, may take you to its lair deep within the earth to show you hidden dreams or potentials of which you were unaware; the story of the Fox may teach you cunning, thinking around problems, and learning from your mistakes.

To find your current Companion Animals, sit quietly at a table or on the floor and concentrate on calling the strengths of the animals to you. Remove the card representing your Totem Animal from the deck, and place it face up in the centre of the table or on a cloth. If you are not using the blank card, remove it. Shuffle the remaining cards thoroughly, then place the first four cards

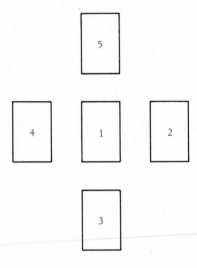

Fig. 3: Finding Your Companion Animals

from the top of the deck in the positions shown in Fig. 3. The
meanings of positions are as follows:

1 *Totem Animal* Your lifetime guide, and representative of your
  inner self.
2 *Mental Abilities* Ideas, aims, plans, choices, decisions, academic
  pursuits, understanding, wisdom, inspiration.
3 *Life Energies* Tasks, life force, vitality, enthusiasm, passion,
  sexual energy, strength, physical activity, projects, action,
  health, creativity.
4 *Emotion* Feelings, love, intuition, dreams, arts, healing,
  spirituality, psychic ability, compassion.
5 *Practical Matters* Work, money, possessions, stability, security,
  property, productiveness.

Turn over the cards one at a time; each animal revealed is the
Companion Animal whose strengths you need to acquire or
enhance in that area of your life. The keywords in the

'Characteristics' section for each animal in Part 1 may help you to identify the major aspects of the beasts revealed. The most important message, however, is your reaction to and awareness of the animal, and you should listen to your own interpretation of the message it brings. All cards are read in the upright position, and should be interpreted in conjunction with the Totem card (the sample readings will give you a clear idea of how to do this).

Sample Reading

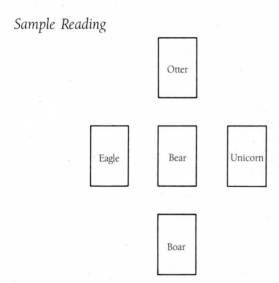

Fig. 4: Worked Example of Companion Animals

These are the Companion Animals at a particular time for a man whose Totem is the *Bear.* The Bear shows that he has strength and the ability to understand dreams and potentials; that he is protective, introspective, and slow to rouse but fierce when provoked; and that he is deliberate, with the ability to wait for the right moment.

In the position of Mental Abilities, the *Unicorn* offers calm reasoning and the control of aggression and stubbornness. The querant needs to avoid stress, pride, stubbornness and aggression in his life, and the Unicorn can help him to transform those impulses into calm and reasoning thought. As the Spirit of the Kingdom of Purity, the Unicorn is a particularly strong symbol, and can also offer the distilled strengths of all the other beasts in the kingdom it rules.

In the position of Life Energies, the *Boar* offers the way to boldness and direct action. The querant needs to become more physically active, as well as taking the initiative to make positive or bold actions which will affect his life.

In the position of Emotion, the *Eagle* offers the opportunity to achieve a higher level of emotion and spirituality. The querant needs to develop an awareness of the base emotions which are tying him to the mundane, and to soar beyond them to achieve emotional and spiritual renewal.

In the position of Practical Matters, the *Otter* offers the childlike joy and wonder of life. The querant needs to regain the delight and enthusiasm missing from his work or practical day-to-day life.

At the time of this reading, the querant was under intense pressure from his job. He had little time or energy left for other aspects of life, and scarce enthusiasm or enjoyment in the job he was doing. The Bear will normally react only when severely provoked, and so the querant has need of the boldness and direct action of the Boar to take control of the direction of his life. By reacting to the stresses of work, the querant has lost sight of the enjoyment and satisfaction the job could bring; the story of the Otter points the way to recapturing this. By interpreting and interacting with the stories of all his Companion Animals, the querant can take on their qualities and abilities to help overcome the current difficulties.

Encountering your Totem and Companion Animals

Now that you have discovered your Totem Animal, and the Companion Animals which are offering their strengths at this time, it is important to develop a framework in which you can encounter these beasts on an inner level and, by becoming part of their story, take those abilities and gifts they offer. By interacting with the animal in this way, you will be able to make use of those teachings and energies to enhance your everyday life. One way to bring the animal to you is to perform a visualization, a process of using the imaginative power of the mind to link the mundane, everyday consciousness with the intuitive, subconscious part of the mind. A suggested visualization is given below.

The beast you encounter in the visualization may sometimes be challenging or frightening. Remember that you are facing an image of yourself. Feel for the characteristics of the beast within yourself, and face the animal as an equal. If you find that you are very uncomfortable with a particular animal, call on the help of another beast to lend you extra strength, or return the card to the deck and choose another. It is possible that you may not be ready in your own development to meet a particular animal; in this case, you should work through the Spiral Path until you reach the position of the animal which is causing the problem (see Part 4).

On encountering the animal, there are several ways in which it may interact with you. Your beast may talk to you, show you a series of images, guide you through particular scenarios, or present you with a symbol. You may also hear music, or the beast's voice in your head. Be aware of your reactions to what you experience, and participate in any way you feel appropriate.

You may find it easier to perform the visualization by recording the following passage onto tape and then playing it back to yourself.

Visualization

Find a quiet place where you will not be disturbed. Sit comfortably in a high-backed chair with both feet flat on the ground. Begin to relax your body by breathing deeply. Once you are relaxed, become aware of standing with bare feet on cool, damp grass. Feel the warmth of sunlight on your face.

You find yourself standing in front of a huge tree; its branches reach high into the sky beyond your sight. The tree emits an aura of living

You can almost see the sap travelling up and down the mighty trunk. At the base of the tree you see a hole in the trunk. You crawl into this hole, into the darkness. At first, you feel disorientated, but then you realize that you are gently falling. As you fall, you become lighter, and you touch the ground by an opening between the roots.

You pass through the opening, and find yourself standing in a forest glade of brilliant greens and yellows. Above you, the dome of the sky is a clear sapphire blue. Everything seems bursting with life and colour. You hear the rustle of leaves in the branches and smell the sweet scent of summer in the air.

In the centre of the glade, you notice a roughly hewn stone. As you walk towards it you see a spring bubbling up from beneath the stone into a small pool which drains into a stream. The music of the water fills your ears, and you hear your name being called softly. Before you, its body reflecting the sunlight, you see your Totem Beast. It calls your name again, and as you step towards it rainbow colours swirl around you. You feel your Totem weaving its story, and gradually your body changes into that of your Totem Animal. In a flash of sunlight, you follow your Totem into its story. Journey with your animal until you feel that it is time to return.

Return to the glade, and reach out and touch your Totem Beast. Allow its body to merge with yours. Being aware of its presence, slowly return to your own shape, carrying with you the gifts of the animal. Return quickly through the opening between the roots and allow yourself to drift gradually up the tree and back to your starting place.

Become aware of your body sitting in the chair. Before opening your eyes, remember the teachings brought to you by your Totem, and be aware of its strengths and abilities residing within you. Make a note of any particular insights brought to you by the beast.

The same visualization can be used to interact with your Companion Animals of the moment, and their teachings. When you reach the glade and stand by the stone, do not wait to be called but instead call the name of the animal you wish to appear.

When you have encountered your Totem and Companion Animals, you may find it useful to carry their cards with you as a reminder or 'trigger' to call upon the strengths and energies they offer.

PART 3

———— ◆ ————

The Card Spreads

A convenient way to identify your own strengths, abilities and needs in particular areas of your life is to place the cards in a pattern or 'spread'. Each card position represents the question or aspect on which you wish to focus. You may carry out a reading either for yourself by focusing on your own questions and needs, or for another person, even if he or she is not physically present, by concentrating on your image of that person.

Interpreting the patterns and answers revealed is a highly personal skill, and you will probably find that your analysis of the cards becomes easier and more certain the more you use them. Readings should be based on your own perceptions and feelings about the animal image revealed, drawing on your knowledge of the beast as well as the stories and characteristics outlined in Part 1. Each 'Characteristics' section contains a list of keywords for the animal's major attributes, which you may find useful to stimulate your own decisions about its meaning. Remember, though, that this list is neither exhaustive nor prohibitive, and you should not be afraid to accept alternative interpretations and meanings that may come to you.

Before attempting a spread, sit quietly at a table or on the floor. Remove the card representing the Totem Animal and place it face up in the required position on the table or on a cloth. Remove the blank card if you are not using it. Shuffle the remaining cards thoroughly until you receive an impulse to stop. If you are intending to interpret a spread for another person, he or she should shuffle the cards and then hand them to you. From the top of the deck, place the cards face down in the required pattern and in the order indicated by the numbers in one of the example spreads that follow. Turn the cards face up one by one. Read the meaning indicated by the principles and characteristics of the animal in relation to the position in which the card lies. When all the cards are revealed, try to relate all the animal guides to the Totem Animal and to your – or the other person's – character and circumstances.

The following example spreads and readings are presented as a guide for your own work with the cards, but remember that different interpretations are possible based on your own experience and skill. You may wish to devise your own spreads, or use ones from another card system. Further work on the meanings and awakening of the energies of the animals identified can, if you wish, be undertaken through meditation and visualization in a similar way as for the Totem and Companion Animals (see Part 2).

The Glass Pool Spread

This spread reflects your own current abilities, potentials and energies, revealing those areas that need further development or

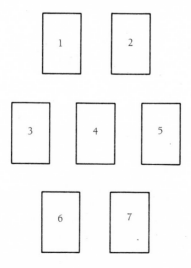

Fig. 5: The Glass Pool Spread

control. It identifies the animal guides who can best teach you the qualities and principles you need to acquire or enhance in order to progress.

Place the cards as indicated in Fig. 5. The meanings of the positions are as follows:

1 Your Totem Animal.
2 The phase your life is currently passing through.
3 The qualities you need to develop at this time in your relationships with others.
4 The qualities you need to develop at this time in your work-related life.
5 The qualities you need to develop at this time in your life generally.
6 The potentials you are not currently using to the full.
7 The qualities on which you currently need to exercise control.

Sample Reading

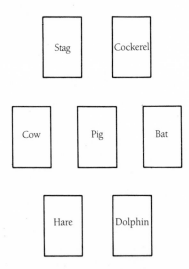

Fig. 6: Example of Glass Pool Spread

These are the cards laid out in the Glass Pool Spread for a woman whose Totem Animal is the *Stag*. The Stag reveals that the querant has the strength of responsibility and self-sacrifice, and can be determined and self-sufficient.

In the position of current life phase, the *Cockerel* indicates a need for new beginnings – an awakening to new experiences, projects and tasks. The Cockerel also indicates a self-confident phase, perhaps even over-confidence and 'cockiness', which should allow this growth to proceed. The querant needs, however, to beware of becoming too aggressive.

In the position of relationships, the *Cow* signifies that the querant needs to become more caring and loving and less self-centred. The self-confidence revealed by the Cockerel may be resulting in insensitivity to the needs of others.

In the aspect of work-related issues, the *Pig* suggests that the querant needs to ensure that her energies are bent towards work and productive projects which will lead to recognition, wealth and material gain. It also reveals the need for vitality and channelled energy.

In the position of general issues, the *Bat* reveals a need for the querant to overcome mental fears and anxieties, and to find direction in all aspects of her life.

In the position of neglected potentials, the *Hare* reveals the need to tap into the querant's reserve of creative and inspirational energies, and to bring these to bear in productive ways.

In the position of exercising control, the *Dolphin* reflects the querant's need to restrain her emotions and to avoid being too sensitive, thin-skinned and empathic in her dealings with others.

At the time of the reading, the querant was badly entrenched in her work with little time for others, and was gaining little reward, either materially or emotionally, from it. Her work was in the creative field, but she was unable to detach herself sufficiently from the detailed mundane aspects of her life to achieve an overview of her direction or to bring her creative talents properly to bear. The combination of animal guides within the spread clearly revealed the need to overcome the up-front fears and to map out a direction using her talents to achieve recognition and wealth. At the same time, the querant needed to balance her own desires with those of others, to control emotional swings and to give herself space to retune to the creative energies. Further meditation and visualization would enable the querant to take on the strengths and abilities of the animals in order to achieve these ends.

The Hidden Track Spread

This spread reveals your current path in life. It identifies areas you need to develop in order to progress along the path most effectively.

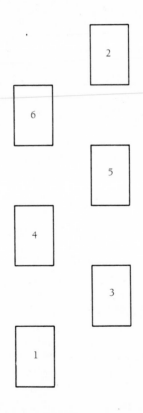

Fig. 7: The Hidden Track Spread

Place the cards as indicated in Fig. 7. The card in position 2 indicates your goal, and the other cards form the path which leads to it. The meanings of the positions are as follows:

1 Your Totem Animal.
2 What you need to achieve.
3 Strengths you need to acquire or enhance.
4 Weaknesses or challenges you need to overcome.
5 Areas in which you should ask for help from other people.
6 What you need to learn.

Sample Reading

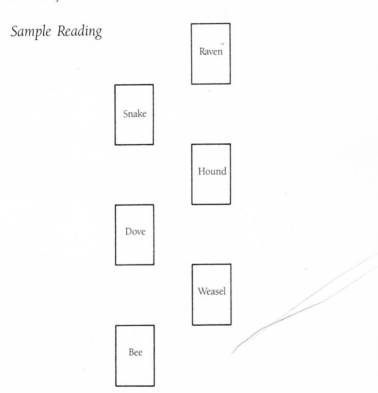

Fig. 8: Example of Hidden Track Spread

These are the cards laid out in the Hidden Track spread for a woman whose Totem Animal is the *Bee*. The Bee reveals that the querant has good organizational and management skills, and that she is a hard-working and productive person.

At the end of the track, the *Raven* indicates that the querant needs to acquire knowledge and shrewdness, taking on skills and information that can be used to her own advantage.

As the first step on the path, the *Weasel* indicates a requirement to strengthen the mind, to take time to stimulate and focus it on the task to come.

As the second step on the path, the *Dove* identifies weaknesses of trust and naieveté which may prove a barrier to progression. The querant needs to beware of other people taking advantage of these aspects of her nature.

As the third step on the path, the *Hound* signifies the need for other people to have enthusiasm, support and faith in her abilities, and the vital importance of asking for and receiving these strengths from those around her.

As the final step to achieving the ultimate goal, the *Snake* demonstrates the need for measured progression through a series of stages, rather than a sudden leap towards the target.

At the time of this reading, the querant was considering undertaking a business course – the Raven reveals her need to 'better herself' through the acquisition of relevant skills and knowledge. The Weasel suggests careful preparation for the task ahead, perhaps through preparatory reading or an introductory course. In order to meet her goal, the querant needs to become less passive and to take the upper hand in situations she may encounter. She should also beware of others taking advantage of her naiveté. She needs to reach out for support and enthusiasm from her 'pack' or peer group, and to realize that progress will be made slowly but steadily. The Bee's good management and hard work ensure that advancement will not disrupt the well-ordered pattern of her present life and that the goal will ultimately be achieved.

The Trinal Spread

This spread reveals other people's perceptions of and reactions to the image you present to the world. It allows you to identify strengths and qualities you need to develop in your interaction with others. The spread is based on the concept of the Trinal Harmonics into which each animal fits, and reflects aspects of the Self, the Inner Self and Beyond the Self (see Introduction, page 15).

Place your cards as indicated in Fig. 9. Each pair of cards, read with the Totem card in the centre of the pattern, represents a harmonic of your interaction with the world.

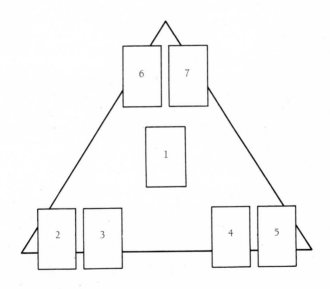

Fig. 9: The Trinal Spread

The meanings of the positions are as follows:

1 Your Totem Animal.

SELF
    2 What people see as your good points.
    3 What people see as your bad points.

INNER
SELF
    4 What you need to accept from other people.
    5 The type of partner who will complement you.

BEYOND
THE SELF
    6 Your own hopes or fears.
    7 Elements missing from your life.

Sample Reading

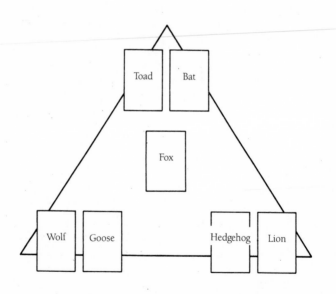

Fig. 10: Example of Trinal Spread

These are the cards laid out in the Trinal Spread for a man whose Totem is the *Fox*. This querant is a salesman, an ideal vocation for the charming, streetwise and dynamic fox, whose opportunism, competitiveness and quick intelligence can be used to good effect.

In the position of perceived good points, the *Wolf* shows that the querant is seen as somebody who will help out in time of need, and who needs to share his knowledge, skills and interests with others.

In the position of perceived bad points, the *Goose* points out that the querant can be perceived as territorial and over-productive, and may at times be aggressive and belligerent in defending his point of view.

In the position of accepting from others, the *Hedgehog* teaches that the querant needs help to protect his vulnerable sensitivities. As a fox, his natural reaction may be to act aggressively, regarding it as a weakness to ask for help to protect himself.

In partnership matters, the querant needs someone with the inner strength of the *Lion*; someone with a strong but not overbearing nature, with a responsible and mature outlook and the ability to be a faithful companion.

In the position of hopes or fears the *Toad* represents the hope in the querant's life that something good will emerge from a bad situation.

In the position of missing elements, the *Bat* shows that the querant has lost direction in his life, and that he needs to regain the ability to find his way through the dark times.

At the time of the reading, the querant was suffering from a hand-to-mouth existence as a result of a bad business deal. The spread revealed the need for him to re-evaluate his life, decide on his goals, and begin taking the first small steps towards them. He also needed to control his forthrightness in his dealings with others, perhaps making his point with humour rather than aggression, and to accept that he needed help from others to protect those areas about which he felt most sensitive. The type of partner the querant needed to help him through this time, whether as a friend, life partner or business associate, was one who could exhibit the strengths of the Lion: steadfastness, maturity and loyal companionship.

PART 4

◆

The Spiral Path

In addition to the ways of using the cards described in the preceding chapters, *Beasts of Albion* can also be used on a deeper level. The Spiral Path structure enables you to use the cards as a guide towards self-awareness and self-knowledge and, ultimately, transform your perceptions and outlook on life.

Many folk stories and legends recount shape-changing battles between magicians, or successive transformations of a person into a series of animals. The battle between Ceridwen and Gwion (see page 114) and the transformations of Tuan (see page 92) are good examples. These represent the initiation of an adept into higher levels of awareness and understanding, through taking on the attributes and teachings of a series of different animals. The system of self-development undertaken by following the Spiral Path is based on this concept of growth through attainment of the knowledge and understanding of each of the animals in the deck.

As previously explained, fundamental to the structure of *Beasts of Albion* is the concept of harmonic triples – grouping three elements to represent different aspects of the same principle or idea. The three Kingdoms are each harmonics of awareness, containing the attributes, characteristics and learning offered by all the animals within each Kingdom. The animals in the Kingdom of Strength teach you how to apply these principles to everyday awareness, or the Self; the animals in the Kingdom of Wisdom teach you how to apply them to inner awareness, or the Inner Self; and the animals in the Kingdom of Purity teach you how to apply the principles to spiritual awareness, or Beyond the Self. Similarly, within the Kingdoms each Trine contains the three harmonics of one of the fundamental principles. In the Kingdom of Wisdom, for example, the Trine of Protection presents the Hedgehog as the 'Shield of the Soul', or the protector of Self; the Goose embodies

'The Guardian', protector of the values of the Inner Self; and the Crane is the 'Sentry of the Inner World', protector of awareness Beyond the Self. To remind yourself of the structure of the harmonic triples, you may find it useful once again to lay out the cards in their Kingdoms and Trines as described in the Introduction.

The Spiral Path is, in fact, a triple spiral. It leads you in turn through each Trine of each of the three Kingdoms. Starting with the lowest harmonic of Growth in the lowest Kingdom of Strength, it allows you to progress towards awareness and understanding in simple stages, with the Spirit Animal for each Kingdom embodying the distilled principles of all the animals in its Kingdom (see Fig. 11).

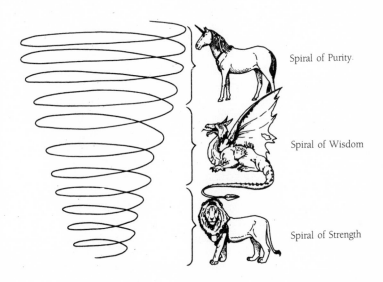

Spiral of Purity

Spiral of Wisdom

Spiral of Strength

Fig. 11: The Triple Spiral Path

Treading the Path

Your journey along the path will involve meeting each animal in turn in a guided visualization, and learning from the teaching or story each beast offers. By becoming part of the animal's story, the story becomes part of yourself. You become aware of the strengths and abilities available within yourself. This awakens realization and understanding, thereby changing a part of yourself.

Different people will require different amounts of time to journey along the path; the more time and effort you are prepared to contribute, the more you will gain from the journey. It is important that each animal should be encountered in detail and its lessons learned before you move on to the next beast. This is not a short-term undertaking, and should be begun with the knowledge that commitment will lead to ultimate reward. The path will not necessarily lead to a dramatic and sudden change, but the final transformation will come as a realization that you are not the same person who started the journey.

The first spiral on the path is the 'Spiral of Strength'. It leads you through the four Trines in the Kingdom of Strength necessary for the development of Self: Growth, Challenge, Intelligence and Creation (see Fig. 12). This Kingdom teaches the path of growth; it presents to the traveller challenges which must be faced and overcome; and explains the need to acquire strength of mind before creating change and new order. The Lion, as the Spirit of the Kingdom of Strength, embodies strength attained, balanced and controlled.

The second spiral is the 'Spiral of Wisdom'. It leads to the development of the Inner Self through the Trines of Awakening, Empowering, Protection and Knowledge (see Fig. 12). This Kingdom awakens the traveller to inner potentials, and shows the means to build and acquire the power of knowledge. It teaches the wisdom of protecting this power, and the understanding of the power of knowledge to protect, before offering the sources of knowledge. The Dragon, as the Spirit of the Kingdom, embodies Wisdom: the expression of knowledge with judgment and wise counsel.

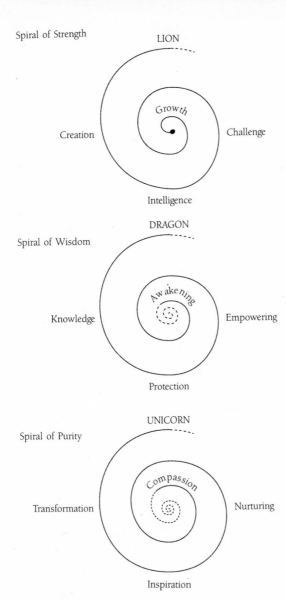

Fig. 12: The Three Spirals

The final spiral is the 'Spiral of Purity', which leads to appreciation and development of principles Beyond the Self through the Trines of Compassion, Nurturing, Inspiration and Transformation (see Fig. 12). The Kingdom teaches empathy and compassion, and the sacrifice of self for others. It awakens inspiration from Beyond the Self, offering transformation of the self for those who wish to take it. The Unicorn, as the Spirit of the Kingdom, embodies Purity in the ability to rise beyond the needs of the self.

Although the Spiral Path is intended to lead the traveller up through the different levels, the path is not one-way; the experiences and insights of the Spiral Path are intended to be brought back out into everyday life.

Fig. 13 shows the order in which the animals will be encountered on the Spiral Path. To begin your own journey along the path, you will need Fig. 13, a notebook in which to write down your experiences, and a quiet place to sit while undertaking the visualizations. The Trinal Animals will be encountered individually in the order given, with the Spirit Animal for each Kingdom encountered at the end of each spiral. The Spirit Animal represents the underlying principle of all the animals in its Kingdom, and must tell its story before you can move on to the next spiral.

Work through the spirals at your own pace; you may find that you will need to encounter an animal several times before you are able completely to enter its story and move on to the next beast. During the time you are working on a particular animal, it may be helpful to carry that beast's card somewhere on your person, using it as a focus to call on the strengths during your everyday life. Before your encounter you will need to read the information given for the individual animal in Part 1, including the Spiral Path Meaning, and you may also wish to spend a few minutes before the visualization studying the card from the deck, noticing all the details and deciding on your own feelings about the animal both from the image and from your own experience. You may decide to find out more about the animal from further reading or research before you are ready to meet it on the path.

KINGDOM OF STRENGTH

Growth	Mouse	*Seeker of the Path*
	Squirrel	*Pivot of the Worlds*
	Snake	*The Path of Change*
Challenge	Boar	*Challenge of Life*
	Hound	*Challenge of Loyalty*
	Raven	*Challenge of Darkness*
Intelligence	Weasel	*Holder of the Strength of Mind*
	Fox	*Mirror of the Mind*
	Wren	*Carrier of the Light of Reason*
Creation	Bee	*Creator of Order*
	Horse	*Bridge between the Worlds*
	Spider	*Spinner of Life*
	LION	*The Sovereignty of Strength*

KINGDOM OF WISDOM

Awakening	Bear	*Guide to Dreams*
	Cockerel	*Herald of Awakening*
	Bat	*Guide through Darkness*
Empowering	Bull	*Power of Stability*
	Brock	*Holder of Tradition*
	Stag	*Power of Choice*
Protection	Hedgehog	*Shield of the Soul*
	Goose	*The Guardian*
	Crane	*Sentry of the Inner World*
Knowledge	Owl	*The Catalyst of Self*
	Cat	*Holder of Hidden Knowledge*
	Salmon	*Keeper of Ancestral Knowledge*
	DRAGON	*The Wisdom of Kings*

KINGDOM OF PURITY

Compassion	Dolphin	*Guide to Tears*
	Wolf	*The Mentor*
	Redbreast	*Sharer of Hardship*
Nuturing	Otter	*The Child of Joy*
	Cow	*The Nurturer*
	Pig	*The Initiator*
Inspiration	Hare	*Bringer of Inspired Madness*
	Swan	*Song of Inspired Love*
	Eagle	*Guide to Spiritual Inspiration*
Transformation	Toad	*Jewel of the Self*
	Dove	*Expression of Love*
	Butterfly	*Transformation of Spirit*
	UNICORN	*The Crown of Purity*

Fig. 13: The Spiral Path Animals

Many of the beasts have similar qualities, such as guardianship or knowledge, and you may find it difficult at first to recognize the subtler qualities which differentiate them and define their place on the path. Some people may need to alter the position of some of the animals on the path to suit their own interpretations. If you are using the blank card for an 'extra' animal, try to determine its position on the path by placing it with the most appropriate Trine for your perception of its major attributes, but remember to seek guidance along the path to confirm this animal's position.

Spiral Path Visualization

Sit comfortably in a high-backed chair and slowly relax. Become aware of standing on a high cliff-top looking out to sea. The sun is warm and high in the sky, and a slight breeze carries the scent of salt. In the emerald sea you can discern a white, rocky island capped with vibrant green foliage. As you walk along the cliff edge, you encounter your Totem Animal by a small stream which winds its way gently down a gully in the cliff. You greet your Totem, and it leads you down the gully towards the sea.

You become aware of other animals around you, and on reaching the white sandy beach you see animals of all kinds making their way down the cliffs and across the sea to the island. Drawn up on the beach lies a small boat made of sparkling crystal, with a silver bell on the prow. Your Totem indicates that you should get into the boat, and as you step aboard the boat slips slowly away from the shore.

Around you in the water is an explosion of fish, dolphins and other water creatures leaping through the waves, causing the bell to sound as the boat pushes through the foaming crests. You see large and small animals swimming alongside you, and the air is full of land and sea birds.

You soon near the island, and you see a waterfall cascading down the white stones to the sea. As the boat beaches itself, you step out and follow your Totem Animal to the waterfall, where you find steps cut into the rock beneath it. As you climb, knee deep in the dancing water, you catch glimpses of animals making their way through the rocks and bushes all around you.

At the top of the waterfall you find a green glade. In the centre stands a white building surrounded by a moat which feeds the waterfall. The building is circular with a white marble dome and open columns all around it. Your Totem Animal takes you to three stone steps leading down into the moat, and then turns to rest with the other animals in and around the moat.

You step cautiously into the water, and wade across to the steps leading up the far bank. The gap between the building's columns is screened by a curtain of falling water, and as you step through you sense that time has changed, and you observe the setting sun casting pink shadows on the marble. In the centre of the building, under the dome, stands a simply-carved white stone seat. As you walk towards it, you notice that the floor is covered with a mosaic in a spiral design, with the chair placed at the centre of the spiral. On the arm of the chair is a small crystal bell, and as you sit, the bell sounds. From the west, the Trinal Animal from the Spiral Path enters the building, and as it weaves its story around you it carries you into the setting sunlight.

(The time you feel you need to spend with each beast will vary, and you may wish to meet with particular animals more than once. Take the time to meet one animal in each visualization.)

When you have said your farewells to the beast, return through the water curtain and across the moat, and gradually become aware once more of sitting in your own chair.

After the visualization, make notes on any experiences or insights you may have encountered. After the first time, you may not need to undertake the whole journey in each visualization, but prefer to begin by entering the moat.

The Unicorn is the final Spirit in the Spiral Path. Having learned your own strengths and weaknesses, overcome the challenges in your quest, and attained knowledge, wisdom and compassion, the Unicorn's horn releases you from the person you were before you set out on the journey. It allows you rebirth with the strength to carry the new responsibilities and guardianships which you have acquired with that knowledge.

Afterword

—————— ◆ ——————

Our ancestors saw no great distinctions between the souls of man and beast, and appreciated and respected the animals for their own merits. True, they used the beasts for food and for labour, for tools and clothing, but they gave due deference to them and understood their habits and the advantages each held, appreciating the gifts which the animal gave at the cost of its own life. Through working with the *Beasts of Albion,* it is hoped that you will have been drawn a little closer to the animal world, and will have regained some of the respect and understanding for a Kingdom from which most modern people are all too removed. In developing the strengths of the animals in yourself, it is important in return to develop some understanding of how society views and treats the 'Beasts of Albion' today, and perhaps to lend them some of your strength.

Select Bibliography

———————◆———————

Coghlan, Ronan, *The Encyclopedia of Arthurian Legends,* Element 1991

Cooper, J.C., *Symbolic and Mythological Animals,* Aquarian 1992

Crossley-Holland, Kevin, *The Norse Myths,* Penguin 1980

Green, Miranda, *Dictionary of Celtic Myth and Legend,* Thames & Hudson 1992

Jones, Gwyn and Jones, Thomas (trans.), *The Mabinogion,* Dragon's Dream 1982

Jones, Kathy, *The Ancient British Goddess,* Ariadne Publications 1991

MacDonald, Lorraine, *Celtic Totem Animals,* Dalriada Celtic Heritage Society

Matthews, Caitlín, *Mabon and the Mysteries of Britain*, Arkana 1987

Matthews, Caitlín and John, *The Arthurian Tarot,* Aquarian 1990

Matthews, Caitlín and John, *Hallowquest,* Aquarian 1990

Matthews, John, *The Celtic Shaman,* Element 1991

Matthews, John and Caitlín, *The Aquarian Guide to British and Irish Mythology,* Aquarian 1988

Meadows, Kenneth, *Shamanic Experience,* Element 1991

Pennick, Nigel, *Practical Magic in the Northern Tradition,* Aquarian 1989

Radford, E. & M.A. and Hole, Christina, *The Encyclopedia of Superstition,* Hutchinson 1961

Ross, Anne, *Druids, Gods and Heroes from Celtic Mythology,* Peter Lowe 1986

Ross, Anne, *The Pagan Celts,* Batsford 1986

Stewart, R.J., *Celtic Gods, Celtic Goddesses,* Blandford 1990

Stewart, R.J., *The Merlin Tarot*, Aquarian 1988

Stewart, R.J., *The Mystic Life of Merlin*, Arkana 1986

Waring, Philippa, *The Dictionary of Omens & Superstitions*, Treasure Press 1992